■ ■ ■ The Triple Victory

Also published by Cowley Publications

Lord I Believe

The Triple Victory

Christ's Temptation According to St. Matthew

A Cowley Classic

. . .

AUSTIN FARRER

COWLEY PUBLICATIONS
Cambridge, Massachusetts

International Standard Book Number: 1-56101-020-0
Library of Congress Number: 90-36545

Library of Congress Cataloging-in-Publication Data
Farrer, Austin Marsden
The triple victory : Christ's temptation according to St. Matthew /
Austin Farrer.
p.   cm.
ISBN 1056101-020-0 :
1. Jesus Christ—Temptation. 2. Jesus Christ—Baptism. 3. Bible. N.T.
Matthew—Criticism, interpretation, etc. I. Title.
BT355.F29 1990
232.9'5—dc20   90-36545 CIP

This book is printed on acid-free paper and was produced in the
United States of America.

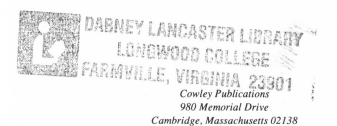
Cowley Publications
980 Memorial Drive
Cambridge, Massachusetts 02138

Foreword

BY THE ARCHBISHOP OF CANTERBURY

I JOIN WITH THE readers of this book in their gratitude to the author for it. It is a book which helps us to read the Bible with new perception and to find our Lord brought near to us with new vividness. We are shown, perhaps more than ever before, what it means that Jesus is the Son of God, and at the same time how near is his supreme conflict to our little conflicts. It will be hard for any one to read this book without being impelled to try to be a better Christian.

MICHAEL RAMSEY

Contents

Preface to the Second Edition

"**S**CRIPTURE AND METAPHYSICS are equally my study, and poetry is my pleasure. These three things rubbing against one another in my mind seem to kindle one another." So Austin Farrer described his creative thinking in the preface to his Bampton Lectures, later published as *The Glass of Vision* (1948). To this configuration one might add the office of pastor, for Farrer was always the priest seeking to share his perceptions of the deep matters of the faith with others for their spiritual benefit. All these aspects of the man come together in *The Triple Victory*: his exegetical skills and his insights as a philosopher, his gifts for expression and his probing for God's presence at the heart of life.

If the phrase "original thinker" belongs to any twentieth century Anglican theologian, it may well belong to Farrer. Some believe that the recognition that came to him somewhat late in life as a philosophical theologian still leaves his contributions undervalued. Those who know his *Finite and Infinite* (1943) and *Freedom of the Will* (1958) will recognize the strong philosophical turn of his mind behind discussions of the relationship of the transcendent and the finite, the divine and human wills, and with respect to the nature of freedom in these reflections on the temptation stories.

Some critics regard his endeavors to identify patterned structures in the Gospels and the Book of Revelation as perhaps too original, even eccentric. But, if a number of Farrer's specific arguments have not won wide acceptance, one still cannot help but gain from his explorations of the evangelists' purposes in *A Study in St. Mark* (1951) and *St. Matthew and St. Mark* (1954). In a sense he was ahead of his time in applying a kind of redaction criticism to the Gospels. He may have seen too many typologies, but he was not wrong in understanding that biblical writers often thought in typological categories. This keen awareness pays particularly rich rewards in his study of Christ's temptations.

The Triple Victory could well be described as a sustained essay in Christology. Throughout these chapters Farrer never takes his eyes off Christ. Nor, fascinated by the struggle of wills natural and supernatural, will he let the reader's eyes stray from "the paradox involved in [Christ's] incarnate state: as man on earth the Son of God must find his way into being what he eternally is" (p. 73). "If you are the Son of God..." the devil tests Jesus in the first of two trials. The tempter plays on the human and finite uncertainty Jesus must experience as to his role. Farrer helps the reader to realize how Satan tries to use suspense and the distractions of anxiety and uncertainty to disturb Jesus' resolve to serve God.

The devil is subtle, and Farrer perceives all the psychological and spiritual subtlety of this narrative struggle over scriptural interpretation. But the steady heart of the will of Jesus is heard in his quotation of Israel's central commandment: "You shall worship the Lord your God and him only shall you serve." Thus, in this wilderness story, does Jesus become the new Israel, opening a way for a new exodus from sin's slavery to freedom. But he does so by the way of human obedience, "by first being a humble Israelite...[in] solidarity with those he comes to save" (p. 84).

The book is full of such insights. With respect to Jesus' temptation to throw himself from the temple pinnacle, Farrer notes, "The idea of tempting Providence is indeed a misguided thought; but it can only occur where Providence is soundly believed in" (p. 53). As Michael Ramsey commented in his foreword to the first edition of *The Triple Victory*, "We are shown, perhaps more than ever before, what it means that Jesus is the Son of God, and at the same time how near is his supreme conflict to our conflicts. It will be hard for anyone to read this book without being impelled to be a better Christian."

I shall personally never forget the daunting experience of having Farrer as one of my examiners in Oxford. And while I can dare to be in dialogue with him again, and suggest that he might have done more with the messianic character of the first temptations, his discussion of evil's last temptation to the path to messianic power is exciting for any one attuned to spiritual warfare. It is Jesus' victory in all these temptations that points to his final victory, through his passion and death bringing new life for himself and the world.

Frederick H. Borsch

■ ■ ■

CHAPTER I

How to Read
St. Matthew

MY UNBELIEVING FRIENDS tell me that it comes to the same thing whether God is taken to exist or not. For, say they, you must anyhow admit that his being is quite hidden away; that it lies far behind the surface of any world we can handle or know.

So they say, but faith contradicts them: God has laid bare to us his very heart. We do not, of course, know any other God than the God who acts upon us, and around us. But then there is no other God to know; his action is his being. His very nature is an inexhaustible creativeness. It has produced all this world of things, and us among them. Only, all these things are perishable. This world, or any other world there can be, is at best the secondary production of infinite Action. The product in which Eternal Power takes primary effect must be itself eternal. The heart of God's action is the ceaseless begetting of a life equal to his own; a life, a person worthy of his love, and able to return it. Hence comes the fellowship of Father and Son, tied in the bond of Holy Ghost.

Now this begetting and being begotten, this fellowship of love, is not an outside shown by God to us men, as though there remained some mystery behind, a mystery which is not or which cannot be shown. No; the life of the Trinity is not the portrait of Godhead, or even the face of Godhead; it is the heart.

5

Do not tell me that the poverty of human language prevents the heart of the divine life from being declared to us. The poverty of our language may indeed prevent us from talking perfectly about this, or any other given subject of our concern. It cannot oblige us to talk about some other subject instead. An imperfect story about God's heart is an imperfect story about his heart; it is not a story about his face.

Human language is, indeed, no better than human; yet no man in his right senses complains because the story he has to tell about anything is a human story, employing human words. What other words but human could a man hope to employ, or what other sort of story could he hope to tell? We do not complain of human speech except where it allows of improvement; and then it is better to set about the improving than to go on with the complaining. If God has taught us to speak of him as well as the resources of our language allow, we have nothing to complain of on that score. Are we to grieve that he has not taught us to glorify him in the tongues of angels? Our story would be a better story, and angels might be edified by our telling it—we should not; we should not know what we were saying. Angelic words would go through human throats like water through a pipe, leaving us unaffected.

We do, of course, complain of words, not for being human words, but just for being words. Only that is when something other and better than words is to be had. Words offer a poor and almost useless explanation of an unfamiliar ball-game or a piece of music never previously heard; we need to see the game played, or the music performed; still better, to play or to perform ourselves. It is much the same with friendship. Words have their place; there is a satisfaction in being able to fix with a phrase the special charm or virtue of a friend we like; but the best chosen words would be a poor substitute for the friend. If we did not know him by direct acquaintance, and through the part of our life we share with him, the phrases we coin in his honour would have neither sense nor use.

So with the fellowship of Persons in blessed Trinity. It is life and action, which to be understood must be acted and lived. If God had given us nothing but diagrams of his three-person life, or nothing but general terms describing its quality, or images and comparisons (however apt), in which to view it, we should be little the better for the revelation. Happily that is not how God has dealt with us. He gave his Son to enter our sphere, and to live humanly, yet still in relation to his Father; so that the Society of Persons which is the heart of Godhead might have place among us, and be visible to us.

The story of Jesus is undeniably a drama in which one of the two main characters remains off the stage. The Son speaks to the Father, the Father answers by a voice and makes his presence continually felt. The whole play of the action turns upon him. He does not show his face. But here again, nothing that could be shown us is withheld from us. No man has seen, or can see, God at any time. The Father's countenance is reflected in the Son's eyes, conversing with him; and their mutual converse is the life of Godhead.

What we are saying is that God has given us a better revelation than by words, however apt; for by sending his Son he has brought the fellowship of Persons on our human stage. Well, but do we present-day Christians get anything but words, even so? Peter and John saw Jesus, they even heard him pray. Paul never did, unless it was in one blinding flash of vision; still less do we. We have the story in the Gospel, and what is the Gospel but words? Ah, but there is a wide difference between mere descriptions of divine love, and a human story of that love in action. Speaking of the heavenly love in its heavenly setting, we can do little but decorate it with handsome adjectives. It is pure, intense, mutual, infinite, inspired, no doubt; we may add a dozen other terms of praise, and remain as far as ever from entering into what it is we honour. But when we read the life of Christ, we enter into it. We too are men, we too have our being from a kind Creator. By sympathy and by a well-controlled use of imagination we identify ourselves with Christ's act or attitude in the narrative before us.

Nor is that all. We do not simply enter into the recorded history of Christ, as we might enter into the destiny of a tragic hero, set before us on the stage. We make his action ours, or rather (as we think it truer to say) he takes our action into his own. Christ lives in every Christian; the life of the Blessed Trinity is revealed by being tasted, when we are made partners with the Son in his very Sonship to the Father.

What I have just written is, or ought to be, Christian commonplace. Our excuse for recalling such elementary articles of belief is the desire to focus attention on a single point. We have counted the steps in the process of God's self-revelation to us. We wish to concentrate on one of them—the entry of our mind into the action of the Gospel-Christ, by the kindling of sympathy and imagination.

In the common case, when we read a human story either historical or fictional, we enter into it by the mere act of reading it. Beyond simple attention to what we read, no effort is required of us; it carries us away. And the Gospel narratives will often cast their spell unaided. No more would be required if all the Christian aimed at were the enjoyment of a story. But he aims at identification with Christ's act or attitude, and so (to use the traditional language of religion) he meditates what he reads. He is not content to let the story flow over his mind; he tries to be Christ in the action or the thought which the narrative ascribes to Jesus. He tries to think Christ's thought, to adopt Christ's attitude. He tries, and of course he fails. The thought is still the man's, not Christ's. Even so, our thoughts, thought with good faith and by divine aid in the heart of Jesus, are likely to be better than any other thoughts we can think. They will fall short of truth, but they will point in a true direction.

Any Gospel scene may provide material for this sort of meditation just described. We can put into our own words what we conceive Jesus to be saying to his Father or feeling towards his neighbour—towards the sufferer who lies before him, or towards the enquirer who approaches him. We may be disappointed on a first view to note how little disclosure the Gospels afford of Christ's inward thought or sentiment. Further reflection will relieve our disappointment. We do not need special reports of Christ's inner mind, for Christ hides nothing. He is not sophisticated, not hypocritical like one of us, he is a person of entire straightforwardness. The inside and the outside of his life are all of a piece; his word is his thought, his act is his intention, his manner is his feeling.

Yet when we have acknowledged all this, we shall still attach a special value to those few verses which reveal the life of Jesus from within; and among such verses the account of his temptations hold a unique position. Nowhere else are we shown how Jesus found it difficult to be good—nowhere else, before we come to the garden of Gethsemane and see him face the most obvious of all trials, the acceptance of open failure and agonizing death. And so the temptations merit a quite special study.

St. Mark, we have good reason to suppose, was the first to mention them; and he was content to give just that outside description of the event which the general character of Gospel-story might lead us to expect. 'And it came to pass in those days that Jesus came from Nazareth in Galilee and was baptized by John in Jordan. Thereupon, coming up out of the water, he saw the sky part asunder and the Spirit descend upon him like a dove; and a voice came out of the sky, *Thou art my beloved Son, in thee I am well-pleased.* Then the Spirit drove him out into the wilderness. He was in the wilderness forty days, tempted by Satan. He was among the wild beasts; and the angels supplied his need.'

If St. Mark were our contemporary, we should say that he had given us a crudely objective account of visionary experience, followed by bare statement: inward compulsion, he tells us, accepted as divine, drove Jesus into the desert. What purpose he saw in his journey, we are not told; only that, having gone there, he stayed there five or six weeks, undergoing trials of some kind, we are not told what. He was in a country of wild creatures, not of men. Being cut off from ordinary supplies, he was cared for by divine Providence—in what way, we are not told, either; only that the angels saw to it.

What we have just written about St. Mark's story is not altogether fair. We have taken it in isolation. A great deal lies behind it in the writer's mind, and what his mind is can in large measure be seen from a study of his whole book, or from other scriptures. But when all's said and done it remains that he has left us without any inner account whatever of Christ's temptations. The evangelist we call Matthew felt the lack just as we do, and set out to make it good.

I hold it to be utterly pointless to discuss what evidence St. Matthew had for the detail he supplies. It goes without saying that if there was direct evidence, Christ alone can have supplied it in the first place, and presumably in the course of conversation with his disciples. I can see no reason why he should not have done so. It has often been said that if he had, his account must have taken a form quite different from anything St. Matthew records. But why? Apparently on the supposition that Christ's story would have had to be as literal as a police-report. And that is a very unreasonable supposition. Literal descriptions of inward experiences were not at all in favour with the Jews. Would not Christ have thrown his spiritual struggles into the pattern of a parable? Nothing seems more likely, always supposing that he chose to tell his friends anything whatever about his experiences.

Allowing for the moment that he did, we can go on to ask by what channels the story passed to our evangelist from those who had first heard it. Scholars have confidently believed that they could prove the existence of writings by older disciples now lost to us, on which the writer we call Matthew drew in various parts of his book, and especially in the part we are considering. I judge these scholars to have been wholly mistaken. We know nothing in particular about St. Matthew's sources, beyond the fact that he had read St. Mark. What we do know is that the Church was much concerned about the authenticity of Christian teaching; and that this Church accepted St. Matthew's book widely, rapidly, and without question.

So then, the story of the temptations may for all we know rest on Christ's description of his early experiences; or, to take the opposite extreme, it may be St. Matthew's dramatization in a single scene of trials which beset Jesus throughout his ministry—and what those trials were, St. Matthew was in a far better position to judge than we are, whoever 'St. Matthew' may have been. On either view, and indeed on any reasonable view, the temptation-narrative promises to cast a unique light on the heart and mind of Jesus.

There is only one way to begin estimating the value of the story, and that is by discovering first of all what it means. Here we find ourselves much more happily placed. Look in the direction of St. Matthew's sources of information, and every door will slam in your face. Look in the direction of his meaning, or intention, and all the doors fly open before you. Nor is there anything in such a contrast to occasion surprise. For, as a casual reading will show, St. Matthew is at no pains whatever to reveal his sources; whereas he does all he can to make his meaning plain.

People think that the temptation-story is highly mysterious, and that they are free to make inspired guesses at what it means. Nothing could be further from the truth. We have plenty of evidence for fixing the sense in every detail; the sense, that is, of what St. Matthew meant to tell us. Naturally, there is still mystery behind his story; but so there is behind any story told about a living soul. Suppose I were to give you a history of my father's mind. I would put it together out of what he told me, and what I knew of him. I would divide his spiritual development into periods, and make the neatest diagram I could for your benefit. My story might be crystal-clear; you might be in no doubt whatever what I meant. You might, however, feel plenty of doubt about the actual depths or subtleties of my father's experience, and about the success of my story in doing justice to them. In much the same way, we may get every detail of St. Matthew's meaning clear, and still wonder about the depths of Christ's experience. Not that we need question the evangelist's competence. It may well be that the most an inspired pen could do over such depths was to scratch the surface. I am not denying, then, that Christ's being tempted by Satan is a mysterious thing. I am denying that St. Matthew's account is an obscure or an ambiguous story. If we take the trouble to see St. Matthew in his place as a Jewish-Christian writer, we can be certain enough of his meaning.

The first clue, and the most obvious, to take up is the parallel which St. Matthew draws between Jesus in the wilderness and Moses in the wilderness. The most careless reader of St. Matthew must have noticed his interest in the fulfilment of ancient prophecy, as witnessed by the recurrence of the refrain 'That it might be fulfilled which was spoken by the prophet, saying…' Scarcely less striking than the recorded fulfilments of Old Testament prophecies are the hinted parallels with Old Testament events. Now to compare A with B involves taking a certain view of A. Those who called Edinburgh 'the Athens of the North' were telling us that Edinburgh clusters round a high citadel, stands just back from the sea, is largely built in classical style, is the capital of a small country where frugality prevails, and boasts a high level of intellectual life. By presenting Jesus in the wilderness as a new, or greater, Moses in the wilderness, St. Matthew is suggesting a good deal more than this about Jesus and his wilderness-sojourn; for the comparison of Jesus with Moses is a far more fruitful parallel than that between Edinburgh and Athens.

That St. Matthew does hint the parallel can scarcely be disputed: the hints are so broad. His phrase 'forty days *and forty nights,'* when added to his statement that Jesus fasted for the period, carries us straight to the fasts of Moses in the wilderness, as recorded in Deuteronomy 9:9, 18, 25. 'I abode in the Mount forty days and forty nights; I did neither eat bread nor drink water'…'I fell down before the Lord as at the first, forty days and forty nights; I did neither eat bread nor drink water, because of your sin that ye sinned, in doing that which was evil in the sight of the Lord, to provoke him to anger.' We shall see presently that St. Matthew's parallel between Moses and Jesus extends far more widely than this; but before we pursue it further, let us glance at the significance which Deuteronomy attaches to Moses's fasts.

The text we have just quoted from Deuteronomy 9:18 makes it clear that Moses fasted in support of his intercession for sinful Israel. He fasted from bread, he fasted from water; his heroism was the direct opposite of the two sins the people committed before his first fast in mistrust of God and bitterness of spirit over these two things, bread (Exodus 16) and water (Exodus 17). We read that in pressing the demand for water, Israel committed the additional sin of putting God to the test, saying 'Is the Lord amongst us, or not?' In going without water all the days of his fast, Moses most plainly turned his back on any such temptation. He simply left it to God to sustain him in God's own way.

So in his first forty-day fast Moses stood in for Israel by wrestling with and overthrowing the temptations to which Israel had succumbed, 'lusting for bread' and 'tempting God.' His second forty-day fast, as Deuteronomy tells us in so many words, was undertaken in direct atonement for devil-worship or apostasy from the true God. For, while Moses communed with heaven on the mountain top, the people, losing faith and patience, set up the worship of the Golden Calf. Therefore it was (says Moses in Deuteronomy 9:18, 25) that he repeated the fast which had accompanied his first receiving of the tables of the Law from God's hand. His intercession was accepted, and Israel continued as God's people.

Moses, then, vanquished in the Spirit the sins to which Israel had fallen in the flesh, lust for bread, tempting of God, and apostasy from God to Satan. These were the first three of the great rebellions of which Israel proved guilty in their forty years' wandering between Egypt and the Promised Land; it is natural to view them as typical of all the rest. So St. Matthew might fairly tell himself (as we can see he did) that Moses in his forty days up the mountain vanquished on Israel's behalf the sins which blackened their forty years' privation in the wilderness: for example, their lusting for bread, their tempting of God, and their apostasy from his worship.

The story of Israel's sins and Moses's fasts is told in Exodus according to plain historical order. The subject-matter is gone over again in Deuteronomy, not as systematic history, but by way of illustration to a sermon. Moses is himself the preacher: he is making a last exhortation to his people before his death. It is in Deuteronomy, as we have just said, that Moses's fasting is directly stated to be the atonement of his people's sin; and since this point is of special interest to St. Matthew, it is not surprising that he should have started from the text which contains it, in developing his parallel between Moses and Christ. Having picked up his theme from Deuteronomy, he goes on with Deuteronomy. Jesus's three repulses of the tempter are phrased in the very language of Deuteronomic quotations: 'Man shall not live by bread alone, but by every word that issues from the mouth of God'—'Thou shalt not put the Lord thy God to the test'—'The Lord thy God shalt thou worship, and him shalt thou serve.'

To a Jewish Christian, like St. Matthew, the bible is as real as the everyday world. Its several parts and features are all in position; and there are familiar paths leading from one to another. St. Matthew's subject—the forty days' fast—lands him in Deuteronomy 9, as we have seen. He is no sooner there, than he feels the pull of the one supremely great Deuteronomic text: 'Hear, O Israel: the Lord thy God is ONE Lord; and thou shalt love the Lord thy God with all thy heart...' The text lies three chapters behind him, in Deuteronomy 6:4. He works his way back to it like a man picking his way across a stream on stepping-stones—from 9:9 (the forty days and forty nights) to 8:3 (Not by bread alone) and so back to 6:16 (Thou shalt not tempt the Lord) from which it is a short step to 6:13 (The Lord...shalt thou serve) which can be easily combined with 6:4 to yield the joint quotation, 'Him shalt thou serve ALONE' (for he is *One* Lord, and thou shalt love him with *all* thy heart). We see, then, how Satan attacks the New Moses in his fast, and, by successive temptations, forces him back from point to point of the doctrine, until he reaches the supreme principle of the Holy Law, from which all the rest springs: undivided loyalty to God. That brings the episode to an end: Satan can carry the case to no higher court than this; when he comes up against 'the Lord ALONE' he is finished.

I do not doubt that St. Matthew saw his way back through Deuteronomy by the steps which are so visible in his story; I do not know, nor can any one know, that he was the first to make that mental journey. The Christian is free to believe that the mind of Jesus had been that way before; 'This' he may have said to his disciples 'is the path along which the Tempter drove me'—making a thoroughly Jewish and scriptural interpretation of his experience. He may or may not have done so— our safest course is to keep firm hold of St. Matthew. We can look over his shoulder as he writes, and see how he moves from one idea to another. We cannot claim to be so favourably placed for reading the thought of Jesus, speaking (if he did so speak) to his disciples on an unrecorded occasion.

But we still want not only to know what St. Matthew does, we want to understand what he means. Jesus defeats the temptations which defeated Israel under Moses. What sort of temptations were these taken to be? Were they very advanced temptations, or very commonplace temptations? Were they temptations thrown up by very special circumstances, or quite typical of common life? The question we have to ask is not, of course, what things were actually like for Moses and his contemporaries in the second millennium before Christ. The question is, how the story was viewed in St. Matthew's time. He tells his readers or hearers that Jesus broke the wilderness-temptations. What would the statement convey to them? How had they been taught to view these temptations?

The answer is plain enough. The temptations of the Exodus were treated as typical human temptations; when Christ is shown to undergo them, he is shown to be 'tempted at all points like as we are.' Not that these temptations are typical of human nature outside the scope of God's covenant. Men without religion encounter moral difficulties, but they are not tempted to 'try God out' or to desert God for Satan. How could they be? Such temptations are the temptations of God's people.

In the tenth chapter of his first epistle to Corinth, St. Paul wishes to illustrate the principle that spiritual privilege will not save us; we must discipline our lives. All the Israelites who came out of Egypt, he writes, were marked by the tokens of God's favour, yet most of them never saw the Promised Land. They succumbed to the wilderness-temptations, and met with summary justice. St. Paul's scripture-sermon rolls ready made from his mouth; we recognize it as the Christian version of a Jewish commonplace. Said the Rabbi to his heathen convert, 'My son, if thou comest to serve the Lord, prepare thy soul for temptation (Ecclesiasticus 2:1). The Lord has passed thee through the water of his baptism, as he passed our fathers through the Red Sea. He hath washed off the Egypt of thy heathendom, he hath set a barrier between thee and the house of thy former bondage. He has made thee to taste the sweet manna of his law, and refreshed thee with waters of life, struck out of the flinty rock; he has spread over thee the cloud and fire of his glory. His fatherly care hath shewn thee that thou art a son indeed, as it is written in the answer of the Lord to Pharaoh, "Israel is my son, my firstborn." And again it is written in the prophet, "I have called my son out of Egypt." But think not that because of these things thou shalt be spared temptation. Fear therefore, and pray that thou fall not as our fathers fell'—and so the Rabbi proceeded with the catalogue of temptations.

St. Paul shows himself to be a Christian rabbi by relating the miraculous blessings of the Exodus to Christ and to his sacraments. The Jewish convert was baptized with water, the Christian with water and the Spirit. So, while the Red Sea remains the symbol of baptismal water, let the Glory-Cloud symbolize the Holy Ghost. The Christian descends into the water; the Spirit, like the cloud, descends upon him. (Any one who has walked through mountain-cloud will see the sense of saying that Israel was 'dipped,' or baptized, in the cloud as well as in the sea.) The heavenly manna and the miraculous waterspring will stand for Christ's other sacrament, the bread and the wine of life.

So St. Paul writes as follows: 'Our fathers were all under the Cloud, and all passed through the Sea; they all received their Moses-baptism in cloud and in sea. All ate the same divine food and drank the same divine drink—for they drank from a divine rock which everywhere met them, and that rock was Christ. Nevertheless God was displeased with most of them, for they perished in the wilderness. These things were examples to us, not to hanker after evil as did they. And do not be idolaters, like some of them, as it is written "The people sat down to eat and to drink, and rose up to play." Let us not commit fornication, either, as did some of them, and fell in one day three and twenty thousand. Nor let us put the Lord to the test, as some of them did and were killed by the serpents; nor yet murmur as some of them murmured, and were killed by the destroying angel. These things happened to them by way of example, and were recorded for a warning to us, upon whom the last days have come. Let him therefore who thinks that he stands take heed lest he fall.'

St. Paul had no difficulty in applying Israel's temptations to his hearers' circumstances. Nothing could be more painfully relevant, as a glance at I Corinthians will show. The newly baptized found themselves hankering after the tainted fleshpots of a heathendom which they had renounced. It was hard not to compromise with the idolatrous customs of their gentile neighbours, harder still to maintain the sexual standards of their new faith. St. Paul is able to remind them that their situation is absolutely typical; the model was set from the very beginning of Covenant-Religion by the experiences of the Exodus.

It is only in I Corinthians 10 that the apostle makes Israel in the wilderness his example of the need to chasten all-too-human desires. His usual appeal is to the *example* of Christ. Christ overcame every natural impulse when he submitted his flesh to the torment of the cross. Though it is not exactly the example of Christ St. Paul pleads; it is the grace of Christ. The Christ who crucified his own flesh crucified ours in his. The appeal is, that we should let him have his way with us, and so raise us with himself to newness of life.

Christ and the 'fathers' in the wilderness are to St. Paul's mind such different sorts of examples, it would surprise us if he were to bring them into direct connection with one another. We nowhere find him saying in fact that Jesus vanquished those very temptations which had vanquished the 'fathers.' The Cross was the comprehensive victory over the 'flesh' and all its temptations; when you had said that, you had said all there was to say.

The follower of St. Paul who wrote the Epistle to the Hebrews took the step which his master had not taken. This writer's arguments from ancient scripture are notoriously complicated: to bring out the train of his thought which interests us, we will give a one-sided sketch of his theme, leaving aside what does not concern us. The passage we shall summarize is 2:18-5:8. Because of what Christ endured under temptation (says this author) he is able to succour those that are tempted. He stood faithful to the God who made him our High Priest—faithful as was Moses, but in a higher capacity. In union with him we are required to hold the beginning of our faith firm until the end; unlike the followers of Moses who (in spite of the glorious beginning they also had made) succumbed to the wilderness-temptations, and forfeited their promised 'rest.' Moses's successor, the Old Testament Jesus (that is, Joshua the Son of Nun) brought the second generation into the land of Canaan; but it was a makeshift business, a poor substitute for the blessed state the people would have inherited, if they had not broken the Covenant. The fullness of the promise (says this author) has now been renewed by a new Jesus, the Son of God. The Son of Nun opened the road into Canaan, the Son of God has opened the way into Heaven. Like the Jewish High Priest on Atonement Day, he has penetrated into the Holy of Holies on his people's behalf. So there is our High Priest—a Priest not untouched with the feeling of our infirmities, but tempted in all things as we are, only without sin. God said to him 'Thou art my Son, this day have I fathered thee.' Yet Son though he was, he learnt obedience through the trials he underwent, and became the author of everlasting salvation to all who obey him.

The author to the Hebrews undoubtedly sees the faithful endurance of Christ as the antidote of guilt incurred in the wilderness (and ever since) by the People of the Covenant. There is no reason, indeed, to suppose that he has in mind anything like St. Matthew's story of Christ's own wilderness-temptations; the steadfastness he speaks of is the endurance of the Passion, and of the persecutions or privations which led up to it. But in another respect he provides a startling parallel to St. Matthew's narrative; and that is in his relating of Christ's temptations to his Sonship. The Father 'said unto him, Thou art my Son, this day have I fathered thee.... Who in the days of his flesh, having offered up prayers and supplications with strong crying and tears unto him that was able to save him from death, and having been heard because of his godly fear, Son though he was, yet learned obedience through the things he suffered' (Hebrews 5:5-8). 'Thou art my Son' is quoted from the Psalm which is also echoed by the Father's voice in Jesus's baptism as St. Matthew describes it; and the moral of the first two rebuffs to Satan which directly follow in his Gospel is that though he is a Son, Jesus refuses to exert special privileges or exempt himself from suffering. 'If thou art the Son of God, command that these stones be bread.... If thou art the Son of God, cast thyself down, for it is written, he shall give his angels charge of thee....' No: though he is the Son of God—indeed, because he is the Son of God—Jesus will spare himself neither the pain of hunger nor the pain of faith; he will, by enduring these things, learn obedience to his Father's will.

A study of I Corinthians 10 and Hebrews 2-5 side by side is bound to make us aware of the salient fact—St. Matthew's story of the Baptism and Temptation is one story, not two. Jesus is presented as the model of Christian initiation. Like the fathers in the wilderness, like the Christian convert from paganism, he was baptized in water and in Spirit, and straightway called upon to face temptation. He was assured of sonship to God, and yet schooled in obedience by the trials he suffered.

CHAPTER II

Christ's Baptism

'**T**HOUGH HE WAS a Son, yet learnt he obedience through the things he suffered.' The principle of obedience is the nerve of Christ's decisions in face of his three temptations. What we have now to observe is that the same principle is already at work in his reception of John's baptism. The Baptism, too, is a temptation story, with the Baptist, however innocently, cast for the tempter's role. Why should Jesus come to be baptized by him? he asks. It is he who has need to be baptized by Jesus. We may remember how, on a later occasion, Jesus actually called a disciple by the name of Satan, for protesting against his Master's submission to the cross; and here is John similarly protesting against Christ's baptism at the hands of an inferior. The Baptist deserves no rebuke for expressing his own humility; yet in so doing he offers a temptation to pride on the part of Christ.

Contests in humility, however amiable, must not be allowed to distract attention from the one thing needful. Jesus does not reply to John in the same vein; he turns to plain duty and the will of God. 'Let it pass,' he says, 'for the present. It is proper for us in this fashion to fulfil all righteousness.' What Christ means by 'righteousness' comes out clearly a page or two later, in the Sermon on the Mount. Righteousness is the duty of a man under the terms of God's covenant. The covenant-terms are set forth in the Commandments. But it is not enough (says Jesus) if we obey the Commandment to the letter; we must make the letter our due to the desire of God's heart, and set ourselves to accomplish that. To fulfil all righteousness, then, is to set aside the question whether Jesus or John has the higher function, and to answer the question what it is that the Father desires, either of Jesus or of John.

It is worth noticing how St. Matthew conceives the actual inferiority of John to Jesus. It is not that John is a sinful man, and Jesus sinless—true, no doubt, but not the thing St. Matthew has in mind here. What that is, we are to gather from the admission John has just made in his address to the crowd: his baptism is no more than a baptism of water, an act of penitence; his greater successor will baptize with Spirit, a sacrament of life. The meaning of John's protest to Jesus is therefore this: How can he who is to baptize with Spirit fitly receive the baptism of water? And Jesus's answer is, 'Let it pass for the while. It is fitting we should thus fulfil all righteousness,' that is, do our whole duty, or yield an entire obedience.

Jesus says 'For the while.' The time will come when he who baptizes with Spirit will baptize with water also. John and his baptism will have no permanent function in the kingdom of God. But the baptism with Spirit is not yet. Though the Christ who will administer it is already present, the signal for him to begin has not yet been given. Meanwhile John has been commissioned to prepare Israel by a baptism of water; and those who acknowledge the divine authority of his mission must see that it meets with an entire obedience. It is not for the individual to ask whether he in particular needs the baptism of repentance. It has pleased God to prepare the coming of his kingdom by passing Israel through the waters. No one is exempt. Jesus is not.

In traditional pictures of Christ's Baptism John is represented as a Christian priest, pouring the water on his head. It seems likely that the form of the ceremony was in fact different. The candidates, having confessed in John's hearing, dipped themselves under his direction. They threw the water over themselves, they accepted the ordinance from him. It is in this sense that Jesus was baptized by John, and that the giver of baptism himself underwent it. Yet he did undergo it; and had it been otherwise, the general pattern of his mission would have been incomplete at the starting point. For Jesus always received what he bestowed and underwent what he redeemed. He who delivers from death died, he who gives resurrection rose from the dead; he who saves in temptation was tempted, he who baptizes was baptized.

The two-sidedness of Christ's action is perfectly expressed in the text of St. John, 'I am the Resurrection.' Does this mean, 'I give resurrection' or 'I rise from the dead'? It means both, and it means more. It means 'I achieve resurrection in myself, and so I win it for others.' It means more still; it means 'I do this, because of what I am. This is what divine sonship, taking hold of mortal flesh, does to it.' Following the same model, and with the same fullness of sense, we might say that in the matter of temptation, Christ is the victory; and that in the matter of baptism, he is the regeneration by water and Spirit. Because of what he is, he causes in us what he himself undergoes.

The water is the visible and creaturely part of the mystery; it requires a man to administer it. The Spirit is the divine part, it is bestowed from heaven. This diviner part Jesus also underwent. It was the act, not of John, but of the Heavenly Father. If Jesus was to receive baptism before he gave it, he was bound to take what baptism there was, and that was the water-baptism of John. But when it was Jesus who came to receive that baptism, there was no reason why it should any longer remain incomplete. The Spirit was added to the water when heaven opened upon him and the Holy Ghost came down in vision on his head.

To write as we have just written is to interpret things by the purposes of divine Providence, and to judge of what happened by what afterwards followed. We believe, and St. Matthew believed, that it was God's will to regenerate us by water and the Spirit; and we see Christ's baptism as the way in which God brought his life-giving mystery among us. We are not to suppose that things presented themselves to Jesus in such a light, when he made the journey from Galilee to Judaea and came to be baptized by John. If we are to look through the eyes of Christ as he then was, we must view the event in relation to the call which set his public ministry afoot.

To consider Christ's entry into the public sphere is to look for the levers which moved him out of his settled position. What is it that impels a man into a new train of action—action, it may be, on which he stakes his life? The question has fascinated the European mind ever since Homer celebrated the wrath of Achilles. The hero's indignation at an insult from his feudal lord has put him out of the battle against Troy; let the others get on with it! Sitting in his tent, he has time to brood; to brood not only on his wrongs, but also on his mother's prophecy, that if he throws himself into the war it will cost him his life. So there he sits. Now what will move him? The defeat of his former allies? Not at all. Let them be defeated. It will teach them their folly in dishonouring their best soldier. The danger of entire disaster? No. It must certainly be averted; but his friend Patroclus can take their troops into line, and save the day. Yes, but Patroclus after an initial success is killed by Hector. Ah, then though Achilles must die to-morrow, Hector shall die to-day. There is no other possible outcome. Achilles goes to war aflame with love, anger and remorse. The readers of the poem are perfectly convinced. He would.

Jesus, divinely born and destined to achieve the kingdom of God, is held in the net of family obligation and works a carpenter's shop. To proclaim the kingdom of God under the empire of Caesar will (short of a miracle) cost him his life, and life is a coin that cannot be spent twice. The hour will call for action, but when will the hour strike? John Baptist, with an authentic voice, calls his countrymen to prepare for the kingdom of God. The movement gathers momentum and cannot be reversed. Jesus steps into the water, and finds himself in the stream of history. He knows in that moment that his kingship in God's kingdom is proclaimed; his baptism is his anointing. Even so, what next? What is God's royal Son to do? He goes apart, and wrestles with difficulty. Then his Patroclus dies— that is, John enters the prison from which he will not issue alive. This is it. There is only one possible outcome. Jesus steps into John's place; Jesus publishes the kingdom of God.

What was afterwards seen as the Baptism of Spirit, completing the baptism of water, was first manifested as a royal anointing. Those who accepted John's baptism made themselves ready, they enlisted in the army which would march for the promised land. When Christ enlisted, he received his commission at the same instant; he had only one place in the army; he was its leader, he was its king. If he was enlisted, he was anointed. The old kings of Israel were anointed with oil; he was anointed with the Spirit of the Living God. Such was the baptism of Christ. Yet it was no falsification of the fact, which afterwards interpreted it as the pattern baptism, the regeneration of God's people. For Christ's royal anointing overflowed upon his disciples. He made them the partakers of his life, and the organs of his kingly action. When he told them that the kingdom of God was theirs, he meant that they held with him the empire of the ages. The regeneration of a Christian raises him from slave to son; he knows the mind of the Father, and acts with the sovereignty that wields the world.

The significance of the baptism with Spirit is revealed in the accompanying voice from heaven. Jewish traditions referring to Christ's time tell of heavenly inspirations suddenly ringing in the ears of good men. The phenomenon had a name, it was called 'the echo of the Voice.' The Voice of God had spoken from heaven when God gave the Ten Commandments; his word had continued the work of revelation through the mouths of prophets, until the divine teaching was rounded off and finished. If the Voice spoke in later times it was, men said, by way of echo—truths once for all revealed struck freshly home and sounded in the ear. An echo of the voice, then, might be expected to take form in the words of ancient scripture, or at least to find its justification and support in scriptural texts.

To understand the baptism of Jesus we must bear such Jewish conceptions in mind. We cannot, however, say in so many words that what Jesus heard was an 'echo of the Voice.' For the very name and notion of 'echo' implied that the Old Testament was sufficient and complete; a conviction which Christ's whole work was designed to overthrow. Christ's relation to the Old Testament was unique. He did not add a book to the shelf of sacred authors, as Isaiah or as Ezekiel had each done in his day, but neither did he simply echo and apply their doctrine, as any rabbi might do. He fulfilled the promise of the whole revelation hitherto given. That being so, a divine voice in the history of Jesus may be expected to echo the Old Testament, in the way in which fulfilment echoes promise, and calls it to mind. At the same time 'echo' will be a bad description of what such a voice essentially is. Who would call the vow taken in marriage the echo of an engagement promise? Yet the expressions used in Church may strongly recall what was said in the rose-garden. Echo has less substance than voice; fulfilment has more substance than undertaking

The oracle at Christ's baptism, then, is an echo of a sort; but it is more, not less, divine than what it echoes. The two sides of the matter are expressed in different elements of the story. The wording of the Voice is a cluster of echoes, a tissue of ancient scriptures, the descriptions of Christ's experience reveal it as an event beyond parallel, a new beginning of the world. So far from echoing the Voice which once spoke from heaven, it rends the skies apart in coming down.

The rending of the heavens is the most obvious symbol of divine event; it is not, however, the most significant. Before the Voice itself speaks, the Spirit or Breath of God descends over the waters. This had not been recorded to have happened since the world was first created. When there was nothing but a restless chaos, and darkness over the abyss, 'the Breath of God fluttered on the face of the waters and God said, Let there be light.' The Baptism, then, is a second birth of light, a new creation of the world.

Now they used to say in St. Matthew's days that the world which was created in the beginning of time had been created over again once already; for had not it been won back from the chaos of waters after Noah's Flood? The Second Epistle of St. Peter builds an argument on exactly this form of statement (3:5). Jesus's baptism, in being a new *beginning,* recalls the Creation; in being a *new* beginning it recalls the days of Noah. So it brings back that fluttering of the Breath on the face of the waters which marked the birth of light; and it brings back that fluttering of the dove across the waters which announced the rebirth of the mountains. For when Noah had his dove back into the Ark with the olive in her beak, he knew that the waters were sinking, and the fruitful hills lifting their heads. When Jesus lifts his head from the waters of Jordan the Spirit flutters down in the figure of a dove. The waters have washed the world clean of guilt; the covenant of peace is renewed between man and God.

God's Breath outbreathed and his Word uttered, rending the heavens and new-creating the earth—who can call this an 'echo of the Voice'? Yet ancient things were echoed by these mighty events, for example, the days of creation and the days of Noah and so we are not surprised to find in the divine Voice itself a chain of scriptural echoes. 'This is my Son, my only beloved, in whom I am well-pleased.' 'Thou art my Son' the oracle of God had said to the King of Jerusalem; the words are in the Second Psalm. 'Son only beloved' said the voice of God in description of Isaac, when it spoke to Abraham his father at the time of his sacrifice. 'In whom I am well-pleased' said the word of God through Isaiah his prophet, marking out that true Servant of the Lord who receives his Spirit and redeems the nations (Isaiah 42:1). So Christ is the Son of David, the king newly enthroned in Zion; Christ is the promised seed of Abraham, who inherits the world by accepting death; Christ is the Spirit-gifted Servant of the Lord, the saviour of mankind; and all these things he is because he is the Son of God.

The Voice, complete with its three echoes of scripture, was already part of St. Mark's story. Only St. Mark, following the line of the Second Psalm ('Thou art my Son...') gave the whole utterance the form of an address to Jesus; while St. Matthew follows the oracle of Isaiah ('Behold my Servant...') in giving it the general form of a public declaration: 'This is my Son, my only beloved...' Even so, St. Matthew means us still to understand that the Voice belongs to the visionary experience of Jesus: *'He saw* the Spirit of God descending as it were a dove, and coming upon him; and lo, a voice from heaven saying...' If Jesus has a vision, it need not be a vision of himself being personally addressed; it can just as well be a vision of his kingship being publicly proclaimed. Suppose the young Princess Victoria to have had a dream, born out of her anxiety over the failing health of King William. Would she have dreamt of her mother telling her she was next heir to the crown? Not very likely, it wasn't news. She might quite naturally have dreamt of being in the street or at a window, and hearing public proclamation made by magistrates and trumpeters, declaring her accession to the throne. As she woke she might say, 'So it's come already!' The proclamation was addressed to the public, not to her; but being sealed away in the private world of her dream, it would have reached no ear but her own. Jesus's vision might be of his royalty proclaimed to the whole universe; it would still be shut within the walls of his head. It was a different matter, when Jesus was transfigured on the mountain, and the heavenly voice sounded once more (Matthew 17:5). For his transfiguration was in the eyes of his three disciples; they, not Jesus, were the visionaries, and the Voice rang in their ears, not his.

It is a question of small importance, whether our evangelists intend their visionary descriptions to be taken literally. Do they mean us to understand that the conviction borne in upon Jesus at the time of his baptism was projected in images and voiced in words? Or are we to take it that the visionary presentation is their way of expressing to us a conviction which came to Christ in some other form? For whether a sudden conviction takes visionary form or not is a mere matter of psychology; it turns upon the constitution of the person's mind, and his mental or emotional state at that particular time. What matters is, that the conviction itself should be true. And it was true that the moment for Christ to begin his messianic action had arrived; it was true that he was given the Spirit by which to perform his task.

Not that Jesus had lived until that day without the Holy Ghost, nor even that he had been deprived of his aid for some time, however short. The Spirit that now came to him was not a Spirit that had left him, still less a Spirit he had never known. When the Holy Ghost is said to come, it is not meant that he was previously absent, but that he stirs or possesses us in a new way. We do not say that a child ought to be left unconfirmed because he has already manifested the graces of a Christian character. For the gift of the Spirit which we ask in confirmation is the grace to exercise adult Christian privileges; and the more Christian, the more spiritual the candidate is, the greater is our confidence in calling on heaven to grant him such a gift. The Spirit so dwelt with Jesus already as to make him perfect in his quiet village life. But now we read that the Spirit seized him, that the Spirit drove him first into the wilderness, and afterwards into the work of his mission.

So the Spirit that came upon Jesus at his baptism was the Spirit of his mission; it was the Spirit of that phase in his kingship which the Baptism initiated. 'The Spirit of his mission'— for though the Spirit is one Spirit, we call him the Spirit of this, and the Spirit of that; the Spirit of courage, let us say, or the Spirit of gentleness, identifying him with each of his gifts, one after another. Because of the seven pre-eminent gifts traditionally associated with him, the Seer of the Revelation actually sees him as seven Spirits, seven tongues of fire, for is he not 'The Spirit of the Lord, the Spirit of Wisdom and of Understanding, the Spirit of Counsel and of Might, the Spirit of the Knowledge and of the Fear of the Lord' according to Isaiah?

It is not we, or our fashions of speech, that make the one Spirit many, and identify him with his several gifts. It is the Spirit himself who does so. His action is like that of the rising tide. The water of the infinite ocean makes itself into the several pools and streams with which it fills the crannies of a rocky shore. Each takes its character and outline from the hollow or the channel into which it pours; yet each of these pools or streams is ocean water, and everywhere it shows an identical quality or power; it brings life, colour and motion to the water-weeds and sea-creatures which are made for it and which await its coming.

The Holy Ghost is God self-bestowing, God enlivening the action of some other. In all his acts of inspiration he remains himself, that is to say, he remains holy; but for the rest, he takes on the form of the action he inspires. As the Spirit of courage he manifests himself as courage; as the Spirit of love, he manifests himself as love; and even then, not as love in general, nor as courage in general, but as the particular courage, the particular love of each inspired person on each occasion. And so, as we were saying just now, he gives himself freshly to meet every need. Jesus had received the Spirit before, but not the Spirit of his mission. It was in this new guise that the Holy Ghost came so suddenly upon him, at the moment when the baptizing of John put his mission into his hands. Under the conditions of that mortal life which the Son of God lived here for our sake, each day brought a need different from the last, and called for a new visitation of the Spirit. If we venture to trace back the Son of God behind and above his human birth into the life of the Blessed Trinity, we shall see a different picture. There are no crises surely, no surprises in that timeless being; the Spirit of the Father does not come upon the Son 'in divers portions and in divers manners,' but flows into him like sunlight under a dear noon. His Father begets in him an infinite capacity to receive his Father's life; and that capacity is always infinitely fulfilled by the inflow of his Father's Spirit.

There is no source of life or of being but one, the Father Almighty. If the divine Son's existence is infinitely richer than ours, it is because he draws infinitely more than we do from the one source of glory; and indeed he draws all that there is to draw. If he is wiser and more aware than we are, he is not less conscious of his dependence on his origin, but infinitely more so. At the same time his delight both in the gift and in the giver is so living and spontaneous that the energy, the creative force of his love is as great as the Father's own. He delights in goodness with all the delight there is, not because it is his, but because it is good. Indeed, self-love is always an artificiality or a perversion. God loves infinitely an infinite goodness; the Son loves it in the Father whence it comes, the Father loves it in the Son in whom he places it, and upon whom he pours it out: 'This is my Son, my only beloved, in whom I am well-pleased.'

The Father's unqualified delight, his outpouring of his Holy Spirit, comes down with Christ from heaven to earth and continues to enrich his mortal condition; only that now it is measured to him according to the need and experience of the day. The infant Jesus lacked nothing of what his little heart was able to receive; the growing boy was capable of more, the grown man of more again. Nor did it stop there; Jesus, more perfect in his manhood than any of us, was pre-eminent in the capacity for spiritual enlargement; and when he threw himself into the train of events which the Baptist set going, there was so much wider a field for divine goodness to fill, that the Spirit came down upon him like the breath of a new creation.

When St. John came to write the story of Christ's baptism, he connected it with Jacob's dream of the ladder from heaven to earth, on which the angels of God ascended and descended (John 1:32,51; Genesis 28:12). And certainly the Baptism has so many levels of meaning in it, that without ever going outside it we can run up as though by steps from earth to heaven and down again. At the height of it is the bliss of the Trinity above all worlds, in the midst is the sonship of Jesus to his Heavenly Father; at the foot of it (and here it touches us) is the baptism of any Christian. For, as we began by saying, Jesus when he stepped into Jordan became the example and the power of baptism; as Jesus rising from the dead is the resurrection and the life, so Jesus undergoing baptism is the regeneration by water and by Spirit. We cannot be baptized without being baptized into his baptism, and the unity we have with him both in receiving baptism and afterwards in standing by it, brings down on us the very blessing and the very Spirit he received. In so far as we are in Christ, we are filled with Holy Ghost, and the Father's good pleasure rests upon us; infinite Love delights in us.

CHAPTER III

First Temptation

T HE APOSTLE PAUL had a divine revelation, which played something like the same part in his life as the baptism-vision played in Christ's. The subject of both communications was the same; it was the unveiling of the Son of God. Jesus heard himself revealed as God's only begotten; St. Paul says of his own experience, 'The God who marked me from my mother's womb and called me by his grace, was pleased to reveal his Son through me.' St. Paul acted immediately upon the heavenly vision. He had nothing to wait for. The Son of God had lived, died and risen by then; an apostle called to proclaim him had his message ready, and his duty plain. 'So,' he says, 'without delay, without consultation of human advice, I set out for Arabia,' the scene of his first mission. Christ's own situation had been different. His line of action was not yet immediately clear after the baptism and the vision. He knew himself anointed king in the army of which John Baptist was the recruiting-officer; but when was he to take the field, and in what direction was he to lead? The Baptist's arrest would presently call him into action, but that was not yet. There was a space of empty time, while John continued his recruiting; and this time was the time of Christ's temptations.

It will surprise no one that a time of suspense should prove a time of temptation. How often, with us, the temptation lies in the suspense itself! If only the situation had been sprung upon me, if I could have plunged straight into action, I should have met no moral difficulty, I should have done without question what I had to do. Worse luck, I was given time to reflect. There was room for anxiety to tangle and for reluctance to build up; there was room for fantasy to intrude between my mind and the facts. For the facts were future, I was wrestling with to-morrow, and to-morrow is a shapeless shade. People talk of the shape of things to come; but the most striking characteristic of the future is shapelessness. By the time to-morrow has become to-day, the scene is clear and firm in all its outlines; every nightmare of imagined possibility is banished by the daylight of fact. But when the call to action comes to-day, and the time for action is tomorrow, the gap gives ample room for fantasies of fear and error.

The suspense, we say, makes the temptation. Yet we can hardly call time to reflect an absolute misfortune, and least of all in the critical case. If we wish to be spared the pain of thinking before we act, we are asking to be brutes rather than men. So the thoughtful man attempts foresight, and the pious man has recourse to prayer. Prayer in the time of suspended action should be, and often is, most fruitful. We are fortunate if we find it either easy or serene. Anxiety distracts and uncertainty obscures the praying mind. The presence of God seems most withheld, and therefore most needs to be looked for and recovered. We have no complete history of Christ's heart while he was in the wilderness. But merely to judge by what we are told, spiritual consolation came last. He began by fighting falsehoods, and mastering temptations.

St. Paul, once seized by the word of God, was placed under a command from which there was not a moment's escape. Though Christ was left in suspense, he was not let go either. When the evangelists tell us that the Spirit came down on him at his baptism, what they have in the forefront of their minds is that he was seized by the calling of his Sonship and lifted out of ordinary life. So when St. Mark continues 'And thereupon the Spirit thrust him out into the wilderness,' the most obvious suggestion is that Christ, having been seized, is not let go. He is not to return into the sphere of his everyday existence until he comes to raise the banner of his empire. Meanwhile the Spirit holds him separate. Since the world of men is not yet his field, he is among the creatures of the wild. An uninhabited country, and an empty space of time, go naturally together. The wilderness withholds him from people to whom his approach is not yet open.

We have no right to state suppositions about Christ's motives as though they were established facts. But try as we may, we shall not succeed in emptying our minds of all such suppositions. Our best safety lies in supposing the plainest and the broadest reasons for his doing what he did. Why should the Spirit of his mission keep him away from human converse until his mission begins? It is fair to look for an answer in the common principles of the biblical religion. We read that a man entrusted with a sacred errand must do nothing else until he has performed it. Abraham's servant, sent under oath to find his master's son a bride, would not sit down to table with Laban until he had spoken his errand. When Elisha sent his servant to lay the prophet's staff across the body of the Shunammite's child, he told the man to speak to no one by the way. We are told by St. Luke that Jesus himself, sending preachers into the villages, told them to greet no one as they went, but to keep the blessing they carried for the households they were to visit. The will of God is to be done before all other business. In laying a command on man, God gives the Spirit and the power to perform it; by turning aside to other matters, not only do we dishonour God, we scatter and lose the spiritual gift.

We need no more special explanation why Christ, once seized by the Spirit of his mission, is driven into solitude until he can perform it; nor even why he should abstain from food and drink, like those Jews whose cruel and misguided zeal placed them under a vow to taste neither bite nor sup till they had killed Paul. For they too, however wrongly, supposed they had a duty from heaven which must take precedence of all personal concerns. It is natural for us to suppose that Christ went into the desert to do something there; to think, to pray. No evangelist tells us anything of the sort. St. Mark and St. Luke say that, being in the desert, he was beset by Satan. St. Matthew says that he was carried there in order to be tempted, that was the purpose of it. But the purpose was not Christ's, it was the purpose of divine providence, as judged from the outcome. It was meant that Jesus should be put to the test; he did not mean to be. He did not go apart to invite temptation. It is best to say that he went to keep inviolate the power and Spirit of his coming mission; or to speak more simply, that he went to keep himself for God.

Such a construction of Christ's motives has at least the merit of fitting St. Matthew's temptation-story. We should expect the tempter to attack Christ on the ground on which he finds him. If Christ were there to pray out the strategy of his mission, surely Satan's opening move would have something to do with that. But it is not so. The temptation is, simply, that he should break into his spiritual treasure and spend it on personal ends, that he who has been anointed Son of God with the Spirit of power should use it to satisfy his hunger. 'If thou art the Son of God, command that these stones become bread.' There could not be a more direct violation of the principle 'Keep yourself and the Spirit for God and for your errand.'

St. Matthew built his temptation-story straight on to the baptism-story in St. Mark, as it lay before him on his desk. Christ's baptism has placed him in a world of supernatural vision. He is aware of a spiritual presence, and divine truth speaks to him with the voice of ancient scripture. Now the divine Spirit carries him on into the wilderness and he becomes aware of the opposing spirit—the Spirit of evil. The evil Spirit takes up and twists the scriptural oracle which had spoken at the baptism. *'If thou art the Son of God*, command that these stones be made bread.' The Satanic interpretation is corrected and set aside by further scriptural echoes. What, after all, had been written about the Son of God in the wilderness, and about his provisioning with bread? 'Thou shalt remember all the way the Lord thy God hath *led thee these forty years in the wilderness*, that he might humble thee *and tempt thee* and know what was in thy heart, whether thou wouldst keep his commandments or no. He humbled thee and suffered thee to hunger, he fed thee with manna which thou knewest not, neither did thy fathers know; that he might make thee know that *man shall not live by bread alone, but by every word that proceedeth out of the mouth of God* shall man live....And thou shalt consider in thy heart that *as a man might chasten his son* the Lord thy God chasteneth thee' (Deuteronomy 8:2-5). Not to be outdone, Satan takes up the Scriptural challenge, and in the second temptation himself draws the oracle of Sonship into relation with further scriptural texts. 'If thou art the Son of God, cast thyself down, for it is written...'

In the first temptation Satan does not openly quote scripture. If he had wished to do so, he could scarcely have found a verse more suited to his purpose than the very text which Jesus proceeds to quote against him. It seems right to say that the temptation arises out of a first glance at that text; a more careful look at it supplies the corrective. 'Are you not the Son of God, empowered with his Spirit, his Breath? Then surely the Son can do what the Father does, and supply nourishment by the breath of his lips. Is it not written, "Man shall not live only on bread"—the bread, that is, which comes from bakers' ovens—"but on every utterance breathed from the mouth of God"? So it was that Israel in the wilderness, cut off from human supply, was fed with the bread called manna, by the mere word of God spoken through Moses. Command, then, that this stone be made bread!'

If the devil's case arises out of a one-sided view of Deuteronomy, it can be handsomely supported by a one-sided view of St. John's Gospel. The Son does the mighty works which the Father does, and is thereby shown to be the Father's Son. The Father has granted him to have life in himself, as the Father has life in himself. The Father gave manna in the wilderness; the Son gives, or is, a better heavenly bread for starving mankind. But St. John's Gospel likewise contains the corrective. The Son can do nothing of his own motion, but only what he sees the Father to be doing; the works which he performs are none but such as the Father has put into his hands, in furtherance of his mission. The word on which man is to live may be uttered, or relayed, through the Son's lips: it must issue from the heart and mouth of the Father. Jesus's highest title is to be (not only to speak) the Word of God. Why then, his whole being and action can be nothing but the sheer expression of the Father's good-pleasure.

Such ideas as these belong to St. John's Gospel, not St. Matthew's. They lie at that profounder level of reflection which St. John's writing uncovers. Yet the lesson of St. Matthew's story is not in principle different. Jesus, seized by the Spirit of his Sonship and his mission, has the divine power;

but that power moves in the direct line of the work to which the Father appoints him. That he may learn the truth of filial obedience, the Lord God suffers him to hunger, 'disciplining him as a man might discipline his Son.'

So evil spirit and Holy Ghost wrestle in Christ's heart for the text of Deuteronomy. There is, indeed, one element in Satan's suggestion which does not spring out of that text, nor out of the voice at the Baptism either. Christ is the Son of God, and the Son may do the works of the Father. Even so, when did the Father make bread out of stone? The Father gave the manna, but he rained it from the air like dew. A small point, perhaps; yet even in so small a point the devil does not simply invent; he continues to twist the word of God; not now the Word of God spoken from the skies, nor the Word of God spoken through the prophecy of Moses, but the word of God in the preaching of John. Has not the Baptist just said to the Pharisees, 'Think not to say among yourselves, We have Abraham for father. I tell you, God can raise children to Abraham from these very stones'? So then the suggestion lies ready to hand, that it belongs to the divine power to raise up life, or the means of life, from stone.

John Baptist, preaching to the spiritually dead, perhaps saw the flints which strewed the ground as though they were the dry and scattered bones of broken skeletons, and remembered Ezekiel's vision: 'Can these bones live?' Yes, God could gather them, and clothe them with flesh, and raise them up, a mighty host. The thought of Jesus is surely simpler; he could easily see the rounded stones in a dry watercourse as mock loaves, put there to tantalize his hunger. What father would treat his children so? 'What man is there among you' he would presently be asking his audience 'who, if his son ask him for a loaf, will give him a stone?...If ye, then, being evil, know how to give good gifts to your children, how much more surely will your Father in Heaven give good things to them that ask him!' Yet here in the wilderness the Son was in dire need of bread, and he was mocked with stones. Ah, but then it had been written, 'The Lord afflicted thee and suffered thee to hunger.... As a man might chasten his Son, the Lord chasteneth thee.... Man shall not live by *bread* alone, but by every word proceeding from the mouth of *God.*' Man, then, shall live, for God will give him food; but not, it may be, at the time, or in the form man thinks convenient. Jesus sees the tantalizing stones, and is moved by Satan to wish them bread. He rejects the temptation, and his need is met, but at another time and in another fashion; then 'angels came and served him.'

The temptation put before Jesus is simple and, in his situation, inevitable. The hunger is in his stomach, the hint of bread is in the stones, the suggestion of a power to create it lies in the recent experience of the Baptism. Christ's rejection of the temptation is equally simple; all he need do is to perceive the wrongness of it, and to repeat the sentence of scripture which the temptation appears to be twisting. 'Man shall not live by bread alone, but by every word that proceedeth out of the mouth of God.' That is, 'It may not be with loaves that I am to be sustained; and though a word is sufficient to supply me, that word must spring from the sole and indivisible will of God.'

To reject a temptation, we need only recognize the wrongness of it. Afterwards we can take the wrong to pieces, if we like, and see how many different principles of right it violated. Then a wrongness which made a single impression on us may be seen to have been many-sided. Am I tempted to take a mean advantage of my neighbour? Of course I must not; poor neighbour! But then, on further reflection, poor me! It may be worse for me to be mean, than for him to suffer a trifling disadvantage. And then again, what of the violation of God's holy will? So we may take Christ's temptation to pieces if we choose, though he presumably did not, anyhow as St. Matthew tells the story. 'What, that? No! just see what it says in the Scripture' may fairly represent the conscious motion of his mind.

The first element to be noted in Christ's temptation is the simple claim of appetite or instinct to be gratified the nearest way, and regardless of other considerations. Not that we equate Christ's moral heroism with the duty sometimes to check an appetite. If that were all there was to it, we should not be writing a book about it. At the same time it is worth observing that the engine which puts the whole temptation in motion is a physical craving common to animal bodies.

The maxim of wisdom is that appetite is not always to be gratified the nearest way. Wisdom is wise after the event, when it has been seen that there are other ways beside the nearest for gratifying appetite. Wisdom accuses appetite, impatient fool, of choosing a bad short cut to satisfaction in preference to a longer but surer road. Appetite made no such choice, for appetite saw no way of satisfaction but one. A starving man who catches sight of food hungers for that food, not for some food or other; the object seen draws the attention and fascinates the desire. The man will not like you if you tell him to keep an open mind, and to remember that his hunger may just as well be met some other way; any more than a man in love will thank you for the advice to hope his heart may be satisfied, though not with that woman nor even, perhaps, with any woman at all. The philosopher may see that a checked desire is being redirected; the heart will feel that it is being killed.

Jesus, indeed, does not fall in love with the bread he sees; there is no bread there for him to see. There are lumps of stone which cry aloud that they ought to be cakes of bread; and it is with the substitution of bread for stone that he is moved to fall in love. There is nothing in such a motion of the heart that is not perfectly familiar. Our dissatisfaction commonly fastens upon some single factor in our environment; it makes us passionately certain that the one thing needful is a direct alteration of this factor. A man is sure that his job is the trouble; if he could only get another, all would be well with him. Or it's his wife that's the trouble; if only she would change her ways, or he could change wives.... He does not doubt his own diagnosis. It may well be, however, that the divine prescription for his relief will leave the wife or leave the job untouched, and move some other piece on the board. 'These lumps of stone *must* be made lumps of bread.' No, bread may need to be sought elsewhere—indeed, bread may not be the answer, wherever it is found. Man shall not live by bread alone, but by every sentence breathed from the lips of God.

There is nothing faulty, let alone sinful, about the immediate fixations of desire. An appetite or instinct in our body clicks (as people say) with an object or a circumstance in our environment. The clicking may be positive (Give it me!) or negative (Change it! Take it away!). In either case desire simply acts; wisdom comes hobbling after, and calls desire to account. Shall we ask for a constitution of body and mind, in which wisdom acts first and desire follows, taking her aim at the targets wisdom has marked for her? We shall be asking if we do for something quite different from human nature as it exists in this world. And since Jesus had our earthly nature in perfection, there is no need to wonder how he could be tempted. Hunger is innocent; a hungry man needs no bias to the bad, no taint of inherited corruption, to covet a loaf before asking whether he can have it. Christ felt the push of desire, he felt it struggle with the wisdom called up to master it; and so he ex-

perienced temptation. He did not yield to it. He hated hunger
and longed for bread in the wilderness of Judaea, he hated
death and longed for escape in the Garden of Gethsemane. He
took his stand on both occasions with wisdom and with God.

If you or I, lightheaded with hunger, saw stones as the
mockery of loaves, it would still not result in a temptation, unless it were the trivial one of cursing boulders for not being
bread. Further than that we could not go; for we should feel in
ourselves no power of making bread out of stone. Christ afterwards spoke of a sin within the heart (we should now say, in
the head) before either hand or tongue was committed. But
such a sin involves at least the idea of an action, and our
willingness to perform it if we dared or could. Christ had the
idea of an action he might perform, because he knew himself
to be equipped with the power or breath of the Father; because,
as John Baptist had said, 'God could raise up out of stones'
what stones have not in them to be; and because man may look
to 'live on any word breathed from the lips of God.'

The sin of the heart lies in adopting the idea, not in conceiv-
ing it. The conception of the idea is all one with an appetite for
the object. Appetite or instinct, jumping ahead of wisdom,
fastens on its choice and, by the same immediate movement,
suggests the act required for obtaining it. All this passes with
the swiftness of thought. A craftsman puts his hand on the tool
he requires as fast as he thinks of the task to be done; and so
the mind moved by desire finds the means of action in her rep-
ertoire of devices. On the top of his mental toolbox the Carpenter of Nazareth had a new and shining instrument, the word
or Spirit of God. The idea of applying it to the present need
was all one with the first jump of appetite. 'Command that
these stones be made bread.'

And suppose he had said the word; what would have followed? The modern reader of the Gospel can scarcely help asking himself the question. He will get little help from the Gospel in answering it. His question is, to start with, really two questions. First, if Jesus could have stepped out of the Father's will by falling to temptation, would his act have carried the divine power with it? Second, supposing for the moment that it had been right for Jesus to bid the stones be bread, and he had done so, would the effect have followed—*could* it have followed?

Of these two questions, we need waste little time on the first. The divine nature does not sin. If Jesus had fallen to temptation it would have shown that our faith is false: he was not the Son of God. The second question is more interesting. We may believe that Almighty Power can do anything that it makes sense for him to do. We do not trouble to consider whether he can make circles which are also squares. The Son of God could not at one and the same time be truly man, and act in a fashion which contradicted human nature. We certainly see Christ to have stretched or extended the capacities of our manhood beyond what we can reach. How far could he have gone without dehumanizing himself? What music (so to speak) could divine power get out of the human fiddle without cracking the strings? We may widen the question, if we like. What could God's special intervention do anywhere in the created world without making nonsense of the world he has created? Could Christ have turned stone to bread by a word?

However hard we find it to answer such questions, we can reasonably ask them. Jesus, so far as we know, did not, nor did St. Matthew on his behalf, in writing the Gospel story. His approach was spiritual, not speculative or philosophical. Jesus does not ask what he could do, he asks what he should. It is open to us to think that what he set aside as wrong would have proved impracticable; that in reverencing the Father's good pleasure he was also respecting the natural order. By making such a suggestion we take nothing away from the reality of his temptation. The sin would have lain in *commanding* the stones to be bread. If the stones had disobeyed the command it would have made no difference to the sin. A tyrant who ordered an unjust execution is not cleared of moral guilt by being disobeyed.

Jesus was not called upon to ask speculative questions about the possible and the impossible. He had only to consider how the divine power entrusted to him required to be employed. The movement of supernatural action was wholly in the line of a more than human task, the work of our redemption. No Christian will suppose for a moment that Jesus in his carpentry shop ever laid aside the hammer and used the Holy Ghost to drive an awkward nail. So in his first temptation Christ had simply to reject the suggestion that he should profane entrusted power for the satisfaction of natural appetite. He must, as we said before, keep it inviolate for the purpose assigned. The word of power must be a word which, though relayed through the lips of the Son, issued out of the Father's heart, in furtherance of his saving will.

In the preceding discussion I have tried to show how Christ could be liable to temptation without being biased towards evil. But, you may reasonably object, there was a bias, if we are to believe St. Matthew; not indeed a bias in the heart of Jesus, but a bias in the whole event, a sideways pressure brought to bear by Satan. If we leave the devil out, we are telling the story without one of its principal characters.

The objection is perfectly fair. We have every reason to believe that Satan was a figure in Christ's spiritual drama as

Christ himself experienced it. For, quite apart from St. Matthew's temptation-story, we read that Christ saw Satan's malice behind the cruel fantasies he drove from the minds of the possessed; and that on a notable occasion he rejected as the utterance of Satan a suggestion offered to him by St. Peter. The story of Christ's temptations without Satan in it would not be the story of what Christ saw himself to have undergone. So much is clear. But even allowing that the devil is as real to us as he was to Christ's generation of Israelites, we still have to ask what there is in the mind of any tempted man for Satan to tempt him with. He tempted Jesus through his hunger. If he had not been hungry, there could have been no temptation, none anyhow in that shape or form. You may believe the devil to be at the bottom of any man's temptation. But if you wish to understand the temptation, whose psychology do you study? Satan's, or the man's? Do you analyze the stratagems of a fallen archangel, thirsting for vengeance; or do you examine the passions of a hungry man starving for bread?

CHAPTER IV

Second Temptation

T HE FIRST TWO sins of Israel in the wilderness were virtually the same sin—'murmuring' for bread, 'murmuring' for water. Only the second brought into the open an evil
which, however undetected, was present in the first, as indeed
it is in all behaviour of the kind. Those who face God with wilful demands and not with humble prayers are putting their
Creator to the test; it is as though they were asking 'Is the Lord
among us, or is he not?' They are requiring that he should
show his good will or his power by performing them a set task.
Something of the same sort is done by those philosophers who
lay down for God what he must do in this world, if his govern-
ment is to pass muster with them as a benevolent providence.
To the religious mind any such approach is abhorrent. Faith
perceives that the Creative Power is positive and good. As to
the detail of the world's management she leaves it to God to
justify his ways by working out the redemption he has begun
to reveal.

Christ's first two temptations, like those of Israel, are linked
together. Here too the issue of 'tempting God,' hidden in the
first, comes into the open with the second. Only consider what
was involved in Satan's first half-sentence. *'If thou art the Son
of God*, command...' Did not it contain an insidious ambigu-
ity? In sentences like this we often, and the Greeks still more
often, use 'If' as an equivalent for 'Since.' We do not, that is to
say, call the matter of the 'if' clause in doubt. 'If you are the
father of the family, why do you let them treat you so?' We

should not ordinarily say this except to a man well known to hold the position described. But without altering the form of sentence we could easily say something with a different tendency. Take the family situation out of which the bible story of Samuel develops and imagine poor Hannah saying to her husband, 'If I am your dearest loved, why do you let Peninnah treat me so?' 'If' in this challenging question does not mean 'Since.' Hannah does not fully accept her husband's protestation that she is his favourite. She calls on him to prove it by shielding her from her rival's persecution.

The obvious difference between the two cases we have compared is that the fact of being *paterfamilias* is evident; the fact of being favourite wife is not. The man is father of the family, however his household behaves; the woman is not favourite wife unless her husband treats her as such. Well then, on which side of the division shall we put the status of being God's only Son? It looks as though no Christian can hesitate—he will be bound to say that Christ's being Son of God is just a fact, whatever happens to him. He is Son of God, though he dies on the cross; a fact so firmly believed by St. Matthew that he can report without comment the blasphemous taunts which accompanied the crucifixion: 'He trusted in God, let God save him now if he wants him; did not he say, I am God's Son?'

Yet the matter is not quite so simple. Divinely speaking, Jesus just is the Son of God; but humanly speaking, the fact is not evident apart from God's action in him or treatment of him. The blasphemy uttered at the crucifixion was not refuted until the Father raised up Jesus from the dead.

Having made these reflections, we can appreciate the subtlety of Satan's approach. His insinuation gains easy admittance because it sounds innocent: 'Being, as you are, the Son of God, command that these stones be made bread.' But it contains a hidden poison: '*If* you are the Son of God, command them to be bread. If you cannot or dare not, what sort of divine Son are you?'

The poisonous insinuation is not pressed home in the first temptation; neither is it answered in Christ's first refusal. Jesus declines to utter the word of command, not because it is wicked to prove spiritual fact by wilful experiment, but because it is wicked to make a wilful use of spiritual power. The suggestion of experimental proof is barefaced in the second temptation. Satan repeats his 'If,' and this time the advice hung upon it makes it clear enough that the 'If' clause is called in doubt, as standing in need of practical demonstration. 'If you are the Son of God, throw yourself down...' The suggested action is so utterly useless in itself, it can have one purpose only: that of testing whether Jesus is the Son of God or not. 'Jump and find out; if you won't jump you can't really believe it.'

We notice that the center of attention has shifted. It was the Son's power (Command these stones...); now it is the Father's good pleasure (He will charge his angels...). The change is very natural. Jesus has just said, in the words of Deuteronomy, that man shall not live only on such bread as man might provide, but on whatever word it may please God to utter. By so speaking Jesus throws the care of himself on his Father. It would be possible for the devil to proceed by saying 'Very well, and how long will you give him? Fix him a time. If he has done nothing for your relief by this time to-morrow, you will know what to think of his fatherhood.' But then the suggestion of waiting out a time would break the swift succession of visions, following on one another's heels with the rapidity of dreams. Besides, it would be inexpressive; it would fail to bring out the full character of what is being suggested. To set tests for Providence is the attempt to force the hand of God—

to create a situation in which you can say, 'Now God must intervene on my behalf if he wants me.' 'Jump from the cornice of God's temple' is the ideal form of the sin—if a sin can be said to have an ideal form.

If the temptation is to be carried to its logical extreme, Christ must be made to exchange the real world for a world of fantasy. He really was sitting among stones which looked like cakes of bread. He was not really perched on the edge of a precipice. It may well be that the country where he was broke into precipitous descents, and that an hour's walk would have brought him to the top of a cliff. But, as we were just saying, one temptation follows another as thought follows thought. If the change of scene is to keep pace with the movement of mind, fantasy must be the scene-shifter.

Fantasy—or, according to St. Matthew, Satan. When he assigns the transporting of Christ to Satan's agency, he means that it was none of Christ's doing; he did not choose to see himself placed on the temple roof; it overtook him as a dream does, quite apart from his will. The evangelist also means that the setting of the scene was part and parcel of the coming temptation. That was dreamlike, too; dreams very commonly build up to a climax which is the controlling point of their whole development. The dreaming mind in its subconscious cunning is like one of those artful conversationalists who steer an apparently random line of talk into the position which allows them to spring their darling epigram. When they have uttered their *mot*, we can see why it was that the conversation took the turn it did. So the whole purpose of Christ's placing on the cornice is that he may hear the tempting words 'Cast thyself down...' The words being Satan's, so is the contriving of the scene.

When a dream builds up to a point, the point is often connected with a physical experience, whether it be a stimulus striking the senses from without, or an organic shift of the body within. The mind seizes, as it were, on such an event, and clothes it with fantasies expressive of fears or desires. The ringing of your alarm-dock is dreamt by you as the striking of the hour for an important interview; it comes as the climax to a chapter of accidents which bring it about that you are caught late and unprepared. Or you choke on your own spittle, and the dream-version is that you are the victim of an attempted strangulation at the hands of a colleague whose rivalry you fear in your waking life.

Jesus is not said to be dreaming, as was Joseph earlier in the Gospel story. But he is in the last stages of a prolonged fast, a condition favourable to waking visions or hallucinations. It equally favours giddiness, and sensations of swimming or floating on air. St. Matthew and his readers were doubtless familiar with a rigorous fasting to which we are strangers. They would take the phenomena for granted, though they would not describe them in the terms we regard as scientific. They would be more likely to say that fasting weakens the hold of the body on the soul. The soul floats unballasted; she becomes liable to be carried hither and thither by spirits good or evil. She is open to spiritual impressions, a state of dangerous privilege; they may be divine visions, but then again they may be devilish deceits, dressing trivial experiences in magic colours.

What more natural, then, than that Jesus's waking vision should begin with seeing stones as loaves, and go on to feel the giddiness of hunger as giddiness over a precipice? Once granted the precipice, the temptation itself becomes physical. Who has not felt the sickening pull of the abyss and the insane suggestion, 'Throw yourself down'? It needs no devil at our elbow to whisper it. Only, if the devil is there, he may clothe the physical urge with the significance of spiritual temptation. 'Are you the Son of God? Put divine fatherhood to the test. Is it not written...'

St. Matthew presses the point about demonic fantasy by contrasting Satan's seizure of Christ with the Spirit's guidance of him. The Spirit is one with Christ's will and leads him on his own feet into a real place and among real stones. Satan carries him, apart from his will, into realms of unreality. Satan has full power to set the scene and spring the temptation, but there his power ends. Christ retains the full use of his will in deciding against the temptation.

It is this feature of the story which gives it its whole significance; it is also this feature which makes a psychological interpretation of the narrative most difficult. It is very natural that Christ should experience in vision the precipice, the Satanic urge and his own rejection of it. But then Christ would not have been tempted, nor would Christ have conquered temptation; he would have seen a visionary picture of himself tempted, and a picture of himself conquering temptation; and that would be a very different matter. Christ must be awake, as it were, in his own dream, if the moral reality of the episode is to be preserved.

An acceptable interpretation in terms of hallucination might very likely be made out. For example, a ghost is probably a creature of the mind; yet a man who 'saw' a ghost might show real and waking courage in speaking to it; he would have really overcome the temptation to fear. But to enter into psychological niceties is probably beside the point. St. Matthew is telling the tale and St. Matthew has not studied the byways of empirical psychology. He is painting in colours drawn from common experiences of vision and of hunger; but the theory on which

he proceeds is one of simple demonology. Satan is showing in-
substantial seemings, as he often does to fasting souls; Jesus is
rejecting his suggestions on moral grounds—not saying, as it
were, 'The treasure you offer is make-believe' but 'The
treasure you offer is forbidden gold.'

St. Matthew's account of deceiving vision may be compared
with his accounts of insanity on other pages. It is often clear
that his madmen are drawn from the life, and that the demons
actuating them are impulses of mania. But the behaviour of
these demons cannot always and in every detail be covered by
the operation of psychological forces. The writer's demon-
theory has distorted his picture.

To return to the subject of our study, here too we must allow
something for the distortions of demonology. But when we
have done so, we shall have lost nothing of much importance.
St. Matthew is not primarily concerned to tell us what the phenomena of Christ's visions were. He wants to tell us what spiritual temptations Christ met, and what principles of truth he
put against them. The setting is (for our minds) perhaps over-
dramatized; the trials of Christ are real. Having said so much
by way of caution, we cannot do better than let the Evangelist
tell his story in his own way. We would not be helped to learn
his lesson, by passing each word of it through a scientific
sieve.

The connection between the two first temptations is not one
of spiritual logic only, advancing from the assertion of power
to the tempting of God; nor only of physical condition, proceeding from hunger to giddiness. There is also the link of verbal association running through the repetition of *stone*.
'Command that these stones be bread.' No, divine Promise
justifies no such action, but points another way. 'But there is a
promise about stones. He will charge his angels to hold you up,

lest you hurt your foot against a stone. So, from this place of giddiness where you stand, throw yourself down and try.'

But why should the place of giddiness be seen as the temple-cornice, rather than as some precipice where one would be more likely to find oneself? Well, if you really want to tempt God—that is, provoke him into action—what better can you do than go to the very house where he dwells, and jump off the roof? Surely he cannot overlook that. Compare the disappointed lover, who threatens to hang himself at his lady's door. Sheer paganism, you may say. Could Satan himself persuade Jesus to think, even for a moment, that God was a local spirit housed at Jerusalem? Are we reading the history of Christ, or the tale of Phaethon? He too was the son of a god— the Sun-God—and he too was tempted to doubt his paternity. He found his way to his father's house, and there he tempted the god with a vengeance. He challenged him, if he was indeed his father, to let him drive the sun-chariot in his place. He extorted a reluctant consent and drove the chariot up the sky. He crashed, of course, to the near-destruction of the world, and to his own perdition.

Christ refuses to do what Phaethon did. But could he even have thought in such terms? We may give a double reply. First, though Christ did not think that God was an inhabitant of Jerusalem, he took the sanctity of the Holy Place with complete seriousness. He can, indeed, be said to have pulled his own death on his head, by taking the law into his hands and cleansing the temple from trade. Second, we must say that in dreams or visions symbols become realities. A temple is nothing if it is not at least the symbol of God's dwelling-place. Very well; in a dream it will be his dwelling-place. It is the same with the act Christ is tempted to do. In waking life we should see it as a parable—the symbol for such 'temptings of

God' as we are liable to commit. Christ dreams the tempting of God as an actual jumping to see if God will catch him. Dreams are commonly mythical; but mythical dreamers are not all pagans.

We see, then, that a very natural symbolism suggests the siting of the second temptation in God's own House. Natural symbolism might still not have carried the day if scriptural associations did not lend their support. The promise assuring God's Son against collision with the stones is contained in a well-known psalm. The psalm begins thus, according to the Greek: 'He that dwelleth in the help of the Most High shall tabernacle under the lee of the God of Heaven'; and the paragraph from which Satan quotes is this: 'For thou, my lord, art my hope; thou hast made the Most High thy refuge. Evil shall not approach thee, nor scourge draw nigh thy dwelling. For he will give his angels charge concerning thee, to keep thee in all thy ways. They will lift thee in their hands, lest thou dash thy foot against a stone.' To any one familiar with the Psalms language about 'tabernacling under the lee of God' and 'making him a place of refuge' can suggest nothing but devotion to the Sanctuary. It is a thought common to the psalmists that the worshipper aspires to make the temple his home.

Another verse of the psalm we are considering carries a more particular point of verbal suggestion. 'With his shoulders shall he shade thee and under his wings shalt thou hope.' 'Wing-tip,' in St. Matthew's Greek, is the word for the cornice on which Satan places Jesus. The Greeks called by the name of 'eagle' the low-pitched gable-end characteristic of their façades. It presented the shape of a long-winged bird standing upright with pinions outstretched. So the side cornices or eaves became the wing-tips. The Psalm places the Son of God's confidence under the wings of the Most High; Satan lifts him on to the wing-tip, that he may throw himself upon the air, and feel the support of winged messengers. The divine mercy may be thought of as an eagle who both covers her nestlings with her wings, and takes them up on her back to teach them to fly. The first idea is in the psalm, the second in a very famous text of Exodus, God's opening word to Israel from Mount Sinai being this: 'See how I have lifted you on eagle's wings, and brought you to myself.' The psalm-idea is echoed by the Christ of St. Matthew's Gospel when at length he comes to Jerusalem, not in vision but in fact. Speaking like a prophet in the name and person of God, he says to the city: 'O Jerusalem, Jerusalem, that slayest the prophets and stonest the messengers sent to thee, how often would I have gathered thy children, as a bird gathers her nestlings under her wings, and ye would not! Behold, your house is abandoned to you'—this house being the temple Jerusalem had built for her God, and which the divine presence now deserts, because her children would not let themselves be gathered there 'under the pinions of the Lord of Hosts.' It was with these words that Jesus left the temple for the last time.

It would be absurd to claim any sort of certainty for the suggestions we have advanced. We cannot be sure what paths of association Christ's visionary thoughts, as St. Matthew represents them, follow out. Yet our guesses are not valueless. These were the sort of lines along which a devout Jewish imagination ran; and the exercise of working out probable tracks and junctions in the movement of such a mind puts us in sympathy with the author we are trying to understand.

Among various uncertainties one thing at least is clear—the devil is an unsound interpreter. To 'make the Most High your refuge' has nothing to do with perching at roof-top height; a promise of angel-escorts to lift you by the elbows when you stumble through stony ways is no sort of warrant for your pitching yourself over a sheer drop. The idea of the temptation, so far as it can be said to spring from the psalm at all, comes from a hasty combination of 'Most High' and 'lift you in their hands,' which together suggest a leap into the air.

Yet however much Satan forces the detail of the text, he could not have chosen a passage of scripture better adapted to his general purpose. The idea of tempting Providence is indeed a misguided thought; but it can only occur where Providence is soundly believed in. If God is not expected to 'keep us in all our ways' it is pointless to present him with artificially contrived occasions for doing it. No passage of scripture recommends the tempting of Providence; no passage of scripture expresses more vividly than Psalm 91 a faith in providential care.

In refuting Satan, Jesus does not qualify the picturesque language of the psalm as any of us modern rationalists would do. 'Oh come now' we should say, 'providential care cannot be taken as literally as that. Saints, like sinners, stub their toes, and crashing on rocks from a height is equally fatal to both.' Jesus says nothing of the sort; nor does he, as he very well might, correct Satan's twisting of what the Psalm actually says. The question is not whether the psalm is correctly interpreted but whether Providence can rightly be tempted. Jesus fetches from Deuteronomy the maxim which lays down the law. Providence is to be trusted, not tried; Thou shalt not tempt the Lord thy God.

'You are tempting Providence' was an old-fashioned way of saying 'You are asking for it.' The suggestion contained in the phrase was that Providence, like a system of electric wiring, could be relied upon as long as you did not make excessive demands upon it. If you did, it would explode. 'Don't tempt

Providence' comes to much the same thing as 'Don't overwork your guardian angel.' It comes out of the same bag as 'Providence helps those that help themselves.'

Such old-fashioned wisdom has a pious sound, but it is hardly the expression of an ardent faith. 'Don't ask too much of God' was certainly not the maxim of Jesus. You cannot ask too much of God, according to his teaching. He does not draw the line between the too much and the reasonable. He draws it between challenge and obedience. To challenge or try out the divine Providence is grievous sin. To rely on God's providence in going God's errands is true religion.

St. Luke in his Gospel rearranges both the temptation-narrative and its sequel in such a manner as to bring out the point. Jesus having refused to throw himself from the temple-roof, goes straight to Nazareth. Arrived there, he tells his fellow-townsmen such unwelcome truths that they set out to throw him over the cliff beneath their walls. A providential check, unexplained by our Evangelist, prevents them; Jesus walks away unharmed through the murderous crowd. Our grand-fathers might have said in their mock-pious phrase, that a preacher was 'tempting Providence' in thus provoking his countrymen. It could not have occurred to Jesus to fear that he was 'tempting God' by telling the truth at Nazareth; since he had been commissioned to tell it he could commit himself to God unreservedly. Not that, whatever he might do in God's service, his physical safety was guaranteed; only that he would not suffer unless it was best for him to suffer, nor die until it was best that he should die. Providence would not allow Jesus's mission to be extinguished before it was well alight; he was not going to perish at the hands of the hasty Nazarenes the first time he preached to them. Neither was he going to drown in the Galilean lake the first time he crossed to missionize the eastern shore. He slept in the boat, his disciples panicked in the sudden storm. He exerted divine power for their sakes, not for his own. Why, he asked, could they not have trusted?

If we wish to understand Christ's attitude we must begin from first principles. God is more than all that can be thought in wisdom, love and power. No one whose main concern (as Christ's was) is with God can admit limits to his action other than such as arise out of his own will. He will not send me rain if he is concerned to give my neighbour sunshine; nor perhaps even if our needs concur, will he send the two of us what conflicts with his concern for the order of nature. An age like ours which has gone deeply into the natural sciences sees God as virtually committed to maintain or respect the normal functioning of countless physical systems. For all practical purposes, the hands of the Almighty seem tied by the processes he keeps in motion; we lose any living faith in a providence which shapes individual destinies. What has happened? We have forgotten the infinite resources of divine skill. We think that God is shackled by his creatures as men are shackled by their machines. Faith in Providence is laughed off as 'anthropomorphism'—as attributing to God what we should do if we were in his place. The very reverse is the truth. It takes infinite God to exercise a particular providence. If we had the world on our hands we should be enslaved to the general requirements of the system; and when we suppose God to be so, then it is that we anthropomorphize.

Science certainly opens our eyes to many of the myriad concerns which the Creator keeps in balance; and we may find through scientific researches likely reasons why God refrains from doing this or that. Christ's age was ignorant of much that we know, and we may boldly say that on several points the theologians of those days would have been irreligious if they had not been what we would call somewhat superstitious. Would it not have been irreligious of them to set bounds to the action or choice of God where they had no grounds for setting them? We may have the grounds in our scientific knowledge; they had not. Christ had an unlimited belief in almighty power; his life consisted in finding the true line of almighty action under the conditions of his human existence. He asked and answered the divine question—not what God could do, but what he would. Since the second question was truly answered, there was no need to ask the first.

Jesus, to be a man at all, must be the man of his time, and work with the stock of ideas he receives from Mary, from Joseph, and from the village rabbi. Many notions were current coin of his thought which have since been discarded by mankind. We are naturally inclined to suppose these discarded ideas are always and in every way inferior to those which have replaced them; and that the mental climate of a former age was always less favourable to true thinking than the climate of our own. We admit that individual men of superior genius, virtue or sanctity happen to have flourished in primitive times. We apologize for the way they thought, regretting that they did not live in a time more like our own, so that their utterances might have been free from those unscientific elements which shock our contemporaries.

The regret is natural, but it is not realistic. The sages were the men of their age; they would not have flourished in ours. The experimental and theoretic knowledge of the present time carries advantages which we could not dream of foregoing. But we flatter our own age too much if we deny to simpler periods any single advantage which ours has lost. The principle involved here is no great mystery. It is no more than this, that the capacity of the human individual is limited. Civilization advances by the piling of knowledge and techniques. The clutter of mental furniture embarrasses the freedom of mental action. To repeat the point we made before, and which mainly concerns us here: our ability to conceive the sovereign freedom and the subtle providence of God. With so much acquired knowledge of the natural systems God maintains, we have no field left in which to conceive the operation of God's free action. No field in which we can conceive it. God has an infinite field in which to exercise it, his power of innovation is endless, and to steer the world without forcing the natures of its constituent parts is the masterpiece of his skill. It was easier for more ignorant ages to appreciate this. We are saved from superstitious mistakes; they were open to divine directives.

The comparison between successive ages of human history can be usefully illustrated from the successive ages of individual biography. I who write these sentences am what is politely called a middle-aged man; that is, I have perhaps the fifth part of my earthly course to run; and my intellectual decay is not yet so evident to me as it is (no doubt) to my colleagues. I am certainly not so far gone that I could wish to return to the thoughts of early manhood. For I have acquired like other men in my middle years a little sense in managing persons and things which I should now hate to be without. I have gained a prudence in handling ideas, and a wariness in trusting my own inventions, which, if still small, are nevertheless precious. I could not bear to be (as I should now say) such an ass as I was thirty years ago. At the same time I cannot be so blind as to miss the advantages I then held and have since forfeited. I do not speak of physical strength or sensuous enjoyment; charming as such faculties may be, they are irrelevant to the parable. I speak of imaginative warmth and inventive fertility. I was making my mental world then; now I have to live in it. I can clear it up and consolidate the parts; I can reform it here or there; I cannot make it again.

So, to apply the ages of a life to the ages of the Church, Christ was our early manhood; he, by free creative action, made us what we are; and the times in which he was born were divinely right for what he had to accomplish. They provided the mental climate for living out the action of free omnipotence. Had Christ been the man of an age like ours, he would have been so occupied by questions of what nature allows as to be turned from the single-minded quest of what Almighty Love should do.

The first century was the time for Christ to be Christ, and to achieve our salvation. It was not the time for Christ, or his work, to be rationally understood. Jesus was the Christ, he was not a Christologist; he was no expert in the correct description of his divine-human person. Such an understanding was the work of after ages, the later manhood of the Church; and our own time has its special level of interpretation to add. It is ours to think out the relation of Christ's supernatural life to the ordered regularity of the physical universe. It was of no importance that Christ should do so.

In looking at our own relation to the past we are easily impressed by the advance of our century upon its recent predecessors; and so we say 'Men wed to be children; now at last the race has come of age.' Such an extravagance of statement is just tolerable, in reference to man's control over nature. Have we not quite suddenly achieved the mastery of our physical home? If, however, we are talking of our spiritual history, then the arrogance of such language is not to be endured. Christ and his days are not to be set in the childhood of our race; they represent first maturity, the phase of imaginative decision setting the course of life. Christ was the man of his age in two senses; he was a true first-century Israelite and he was a true thirty-year-old. He was never a middle-aged, still less an ageing man; he left to the Church's after history the phases of thought and experience proper to advancing years.

Our comparison between the ages of history and the ages of a single life is no better than a parable. If my readers find it farfetched or unhelpful, let them write it off. Perhaps there was no need to labour the point, that the 'unscientific' character of Christ's mental world served the divine purpose best. Perhaps we are too sensible to worry because Christ did not do for us what we can do so well for ourselves. We can put in all the science that is needed; it's our strong point, is it not?

Our problem of Christ's knowledge would, indeed, be a simple matter if it concerned only his acquaintance or non-acquaintance with modern theories and modern discoveries. In fact, the question goes deeper; it concerns Christ's certainty of his Sonship to God. If Christ was what faith takes him to be, how could he fail to know what he was? Yet St. Matthew's story implies that the temptation to prove divine Sonship by violent experiment was a real temptation to Christ. And no one would be so tempted who already had certain knowledge of the fact to be tested. Try to conceive yourself tempted to prove at serious risk to yourself something of which you are perfectly assured. 'Veto everything the College statutes empower you to veto, and then you will know whether you are really the President of the College.' 'But I *am* the President; there is no sense in my endangering my position in order to prove that I hold it.' If Christ similarly knew that he was the Son of God, how could he be tempted by Satan's suggested proof? He rejected it, indeed; but the episode loses all moral importance if, in doing so, he was brushing off a mere absurdity.

No orthodox Christian will doubt that Christ's certainty was as firm as it could be; but how firm was that? You cannot have certainty about an issue unless the issue is tolerably clear. Whether one is, or is not, President of the College is a perfectly clear issue; there is no mystery as to what the status is, nor how a man comes to hold it. And so we suppose that there is a set status, God the Son Incarnate, and that Jesus had only to ask himself whether he held it or not. In fact, Jesus could not ask himself any such question; the very phrases in which to pose it were non-existent. There was no such notion as 'God the Son' or 'God-made-man.' The terms were later invented, and the ideas formed, to describe what Jesus had shown himself to be. He had to find his own way into being it, and without the aid of such ideas or terms.

I am not preaching heresy. Jesus did not have to become the divine Son of God; he was the Son of God from all eternity. He had to realize and to live out what he was in terms of human life. He was Son of God from birth—he was Son of God from his conception in the womb. But lying in the cradle he had as yet achieved no realization of what he was. Do you suppose that Mary confided to Jesus the secret of a miraculous birth? If so, how old would he need to be before he would understand a word that she said? And when he did understand it, what would it tell him about himself? He was a child in whose begetting divine assistance had done more even than in Isaac's; and so he was doubtless marked to play a decisive part in the life of God's people. But what part would that be?

'Obviously' it will be said 'the part of Messiah. Was not all Israel looking for Messiah to come?' Yes, the expectation was widespread, if not exactly universal. But the whole function of King Messiah was that he should come with power and reign. Jesus found himself called to be Messiah when his hand grasped neither the scepter nor the sword. The scepter was not within his reach; and as for taking the sword, Jesus could not see the way of God as the way of violence. What then did it mean to be Messiah and Son of God?

Without pushing the mystery any further, we have said enough to show that Christ's conviction of unique status could not be a piece of simple knowledge. It was nothing like knowing that you are the son of William and Jane Robinson or that you are the Mayor of Casterbridge. It was something into which Jesus was finding his way, something he was realizing in living it out. And surely under these conditions the temptation of a short cut to knowledge was most vivid and besetting.

According to St. Matthew's story the issue turns on 'Son of God.' The baptism-voice has assured Jesus that the title is his. As a byname for Messiah it would express power and privilege. Should not Messiah, being 'Son of God,' enjoy the free exercise of supernatural gifts? Might not he presume to approach God on a special footing, and do what would be presumption for other men, in putting divine Fatherhood to the test? Jesus's answer is to place himself firmly under the Law of Religion. To be the Son of God is to be perfect in obedience. Trust, not test, is the rule of faith. Divine Sonship is not an advantage held by the son of the householder over the household servants. It is filial devotion to the Father of the house. Since the Father's law is the Father's desire, the Son will be above all forward to fulfil it. Christ takes to himself what was said to Israel: Thou shalt not tempt the Lord thy God.

So Christ sets out to learn his Sonship through patience and submission; what the Almighty Will does through him shows what he is. It is a terrible thing when the rigidity of a supposed orthodoxy robs Christians of a precious truth, the truth that Jesus lived like us the life of faith; when they imagine him to have had so flat a certainty, that 'If thou art the Son of God' could insinuate no real temptation. Who walks more by faith, or more by sight—the Jesus of the Gospel, or his modern disciple? Jesus wrestled with a mystery far more baffling than any we are required to explore: he was called upon to be the Son of God in the world, when it was still unknown what it meant to be that. He had a brighter light in his own heart than we have in ours; for he had all candour and all good will, and he had the Holy Ghost. We, on the other hand, have far dearer waymarks on the road we are to tread; we have all the beacons he lighted and left us in his passage through the world.

CHAPTER V

Third Temptation

L EFT TO OUR own wits, we might have expected Satan's attempts on Christ to become progressively more subtle. If a gross temptation has failed to beguile a holy soul, what hope is there that a grosser will succeed? The tempter will want to try something more ingeniously disguised. We may recall Eliot's play, where the last temptation is also the most insidious: 'to do the right thing for the wrong reason.' Not only is this the sort of strategy we expect the fiend to adopt; it is the sort of story we read in the lives of saints. Satan abandons the hope of catching them with carnal bait. As they advance in holiness he keeps pace with them, and centers their temptations where their aspirations lie.

Never mind what common form, or what Satanic cunning might lead us to expect; for it is dear that Christ's temptations, so far from being progressively better disguised, grow progressively more outrageous. 'Use your supernatural power to meet your extreme need.' Fair enough, perhaps; why not use God-given abilities to preserve oneself for God-given work? 'Commit what will be a suicide unless God intervenes.' Surely not; trying God out is gross impiety, and condemned in scripture. 'Worship the devil and have the world.' Nothing more monstrous could be suggested; is not an undivided loyalty to God the first law of religion?

How are we to explain an order of development so opposite to what we expect? We shall be driven to scrutinize our expectations. Perhaps the comparisons on which we based them were not so relevant as we supposed. After all, Christ's temptations are not those of successive decades in a man's life; all three pass in a moment. They are not even the product of three successive occasions; if they were, Satan might choose more and more subtle approaches. They are the development of a single situation, the three phases of one temptation. To satisfy appetite by the use of entrusted power might be innocent if the power had been entrusted for any such purpose. What else can Satan suggest? Why, to blackmail God. But then that's so utterly irreligious. Very well then, address your request to a more appropriate quarter; everything in the world can be had from the prince of the world. Ah, but that's downright apostasy!

As in the story of Job, Satan is free to do his worst; his victim is in his hand. He can take him anywhere, show him anything, make any suggestion he likes. Yet the activity of Satan serves the providence of God. The Spirit led Jesus into the wilderness to the end that he might undergo temptation; and Satan's freedom, employed against the Son of God, can achieve nothing but Satan's exposure and downfall. Jesus can be physically hallucinated, he cannot be morally deceived. The more relentlessly the temptation is pressed, the more certain it is to come out in its true colours. The final temptation is the temptation to worship God's enemy. And what else could it be? Once the issues have been clarified, every temptation we ever experience comes down to that. If it has once been seen that the Will of God is against the thing we are moved to do, then it is plain that we are being tempted to throw off our allegiance. It was impossible for Christ to miss so evident a truth. It was equally impossible for the temptation to tempt him any longer once he had perceived it. Satan was finished. 'Depart from me, Satan, for it is written, The Lord thy God shalt thou worship and him only serve.' Satan went without another word.

Up to this final point, we do not even know whether the
identity of his tempter is disclosed to Jesus. Suggestions are
presented, visions are shown; the person of Satan features in
neither. The third vision itself is not a vision of Satan, it is a vision of the world's kingdoms. It is only when temptation
speaks for the last time that the tempter's person is thrown into
the scale. He speaks no longer of what Jesus might do, being
the Son of God, nor of what God will do, if Jesus is his Son.
He speaks of what he will do himself, if Jesus will adore him.
'All these things will I give thee, if thou wilt fall down and
worship me.' There is scarcely a doubt possible over the identity of the spirit who says such a thing as this. If he is not
Satan, he is a spirit of Satan. When this temptation is rejected,
Satan is rejected, for Satan has offered himself. He is banished
from the presence and he goes.

There is, then, a climax of evil in the three temptations. A
climax—and 'climax' originally meant 'steps up and up.' In
modern minds, I suppose, the original metaphor has been sup-
planted by another. When we say 'climax' we think of an in-
tensity stretched to breaking-point; we speak of an emotional
excitement, a political crisis, or an infectious fever as nearing
its climax. Even so, we speak of a *mounting* tension; so the figure of the climbing steps is not gone beyond recall. That the
three temptations form a climax in the ancient sense, a ladder
ascending, is obvious. In the first of them Christ is on the
ground. In the second he is on the roof of the Temple. In the
third he is on the roof of the world.

Christ is lifted up and up. Now 'lifting up' in biblical language is a symbol with a double sense. God lifts men up and
sets them on high; he not only gives them glory and power, he
brings them near to himself, in the high and holy place where
he dwells. The supreme example is Christ's own ascension.

But the way to such a blessed uplifting is through abasement. It is those who deflate themselves of all pretension and sink to the level of their true condition that God lifts up. Those who lift themselves up, or are exalted by any hand other than the divine, get above themselves and are ripe for a fall. So it became a piece of traditional lore in later times that divine influences make us calm and humble, while diabolic suggestions lift us up and excite us. And so, say the masters of the spiritual life, if our seeming 'inspirations' have an uplifting effect on us, we had better think twice before we follow them.

It is not surprising, therefore, that Satan should do to Christ in fantasy what in moral reality he would like to do to him and cannot—to lift him higher and higher into the air. In so doing, he undeniably lifts him farther and farther from real ground. Christ really sat among the stones that looked like loaves. He did not really perch on the cornice of the Temple; but the Temple was at least a real building not very many miles away, it had a cornice where a man could stand, and for one so placed the downward leap would have an all too real fascination. But as for the mountain of the last temptation, not only was it false that Christ was there, it was not true that there was any such place for him to be. There never was a peak anywhere from which all the kingdoms of the world could be overlooked.

When we were examining the first temptation, we saw how naturally it grew out of the Baptism-Vision; and then, moving forward, we saw how the second temptation developed from seeds planted by the first. It does not seem likely that the continuity should break between the second and the last. What links, then, of word or of image can we observe? We may call the up-and-up lifting of Christ by Satan a continuity of image, and it receives verbal support from the formula. 'Then the devil taketh him to...Again the devil taketh him to...' Still, of itself it does not give us much. Satan will carry Christ to a still higher eminence than the temple-roof. But why should this yet higher eminence have the special character of viewpoint for a panorama of kingdoms? If we are to see the last temptation as growing out of the second, we want to trace from there the source of the kingdom-idea.

Before we make our enquiry, we had better give ourselves a caution. It is no use our trying to make out that the last two items in our series are as closely linked as either of the two pairs preceding them. There is more of a gap or leap before the last temptation, and naturally enough. The Voice at the Baptism introduced the theme 'Son of God Only Beloved' and the first two temptations took it up. For 'Son of God' is a relationship running in two directions, and the two temptations probe it, facing first the one way, and then the other. The relationship places divine powers in the Son; let him exert them. It promises special providences from the Father; let Jesus invoke them. The probe has been pushed in both directions; the experiment is in so far complete. If temptation is to break along a third line it must break out of the Father-Son relation. And so in fact we find. The third temptation does not follow the former two in using the introductory phrase, 'If thou art the Son of God.' It comes straight to the proposal with 'All this will I give thee.' The change of form fits the logic of the thought. Since the temptation to exploit the Father-Son relationship has been exhausted, it remains for Satan to come forward with an offer of his own.

Naturally, the devil offers Jesus all he has to give, or all he can pretend he has. Since there is nothing to recommend the giver, he must stake his chances on the gift. There is no attraction in 'Worship Satan,' for Satan is not worshipful. But 'All the kingdoms of the world and their glory,' here's something, surely; and all to be had by giving the devil his due. The single-minded service of God is our duty in its own sphere. When you have seen how utterly pure and spiritual it is, you realize that practical politics must be conducted on other principles. You can't use your God-given status to meet earthly requirements, you can't hasten the hand of God to help you out. What then? You will undoubtedly look elsewhere. Worship God—yes, of course; why not? But give Mammon his shilling. We all do, don't we? We are all men of the world.

Yes, but 'All the kingdoms of the world and the glory of them.' That's a far cry, surely, from a bit of bread—from the loaf which the stone so cruelly suggested, and which set temptation in motion. A far cry, indeed, but how typical of temptation! How common it is, for the tempter to disguise the simplicity of the choice before us by spreading and magnifying the issue! 'The man's rude,' says reason, 'but he's tired. Don't take it up with him.' 'But,' resentment answers, 'I can't let it pass; my whole relation with the man is affected. If I don't put it straight, I shall be on a false footing with him for ever.' 'Oh, come now,' says reason, 'you don't really believe what you say. John isn't such a tough specimen as that. Be patient, and he'll come round. You'll only delay the process by rubbing him up.' 'That might do,' says resentment, 'if it were only a matter of John and me, but there's the principle of the thing. If people are to get away with aggressiveness, good-bye to civilized existence.'

It is not difficult to rephrase the temptation of Christ in a way which will bring out a similar pattern. 'You're starving!' Yes, I know. I hope I shall get at some food soon. 'Soon? Why not now? Don't you see that the truth of the Divine Voice is at stake? How can you claim to be the Son of God, and not have a word of power by which to satisfy your need?' The word of power must come from the mouth of God. I do not doubt that it will. 'Very well, throw yourself on God's providence, prove the truth of what you have been told; make a decisive experiment.' But that would be *tempting God*. 'Ah, I'd forgotten that. It's against the rules of religion; they debar you, don't they, from pressing home any demand relating to earthly things? There's no thoroughfare into the kingdoms or glories of the world through the service of God. But the barrier is quite artificial; a few concessions in another direction, a commonsense homage to what all men recognize, and the road is open.'

We observe that the same trick is tried twice. First the issue is enlarged from 'What shall you eat?' to 'Are you the Son of God?', and second from necessities (a bite of bread) to superfluities (all the kingdoms of the world and their glory). The trick is certainly an old one according to the Bible story. Hearing that one tree in Paradise was forbidden to our first parents, 'What is this commandment of God,' said the serpent to Eve, 'forbidding you to eat from any tree in the orchard?' From one tree to a hundred trees, from a loaf of bread to the riches of empire: so it is that temptation magnifies the issue.

But when we have shown that wide screens and panoramic shots are the stock-in-trade of Satanic illusion, we have still not explained why on this occasion the picture should be a mountaintop vista of earthly kingdoms. Let us try again.

Jesus has twice quoted Deuteronomy against Satan. The situation of Israel in the wilderness is evidently understood by St. Matthew to be in Christ's mind, and he no less evidently intends it to be in the minds of his readers. We have seen Christ vanquish the first two temptations of Israel, lusting for bread and tempting God: we see that his next battle must be with the third, that of devil worship or idolatry. Now according to the

Exodus story, the occasion of the third temptation was not physical need; it was loss of patience. And it was the progress of their expedition about which the people felt so frustrated. They had come up out of Egypt to go and possess the kingdoms of Canaan. Moses had brought them as far as Sinai in the wilderness, but now Moses had vanished into the mountain-top for his forty day fast. It was religion, no doubt, but it wasn't politics. What was happening to the expedition? How long were the tribes to wait? They said to Aaron, 'Up, make us a god to lead us on. As for this Moses who brought us out of Egypt, we know not what is become of him.' So Aaron asked for the women's earrings, and made them into a golden calf. 'Here, O Israel,' said he, 'is your god who has brought you up out of Egypt.' They worshipped and offered sacrifice.

The false god was to lead them on. He held out the promise of continuing the march and annexing the kingdoms. The leadership of Aaron and the golden calf was to be a substitute for the leadership of the Lord through Moses. What justification was there for the people's impatience? Suppose they could have read the future, suppose they could have known what Moses would do with them when he came back to them, would they have seen their anxiety to be groundless? Would they have seen Moses lead them victoriously into the promised lands? They would not. He who kept them waiting forty days beneath Sinai was going to keep them waiting forty years in the desert; for excellent and religious reasons, no doubt. So their children were going to possess the kingdoms, they were not; their carcasses were to fall in the wilderness. Not even Moses was to be exempt. At the end of the forty years he was going to climb another mountain; he was to survey Canaan from the Moabite border in the sweep of a single view. The divine voice would speak in his ears, and it would say: 'This is the land which I swore unto Abraham, Isaac and Jacob saying, I will give it unto thy seed. I have caused thee to see it with thine eyes, but thou shalt not go over thither.'

So then the false god, the calf of gold, embodies the false promise of a short cut to the possession of kingdoms; of kingdoms seen from the mountain-top afar, and withheld by God from his children behind the barrier of death.

Now to compare the situation of Jesus. The second temptation has applied to him the promises of the ninety-first psalm. When considering the bearings of psalm-quotations, we have to remember that no one in New Testament times doubted for a moment that the psalms were either written by David, or addressed to him. So it is David to whom it is said, 'He shall give his angels charge of thee...they shall raise thee on their hands...' David, or the heir of his name, his kingdom and his blessing. The family of David having ceased for the while to reign, the 'sure mercies covenanted to David' were in abeyance; but 'David' would reappear to claim them in the person of King Messiah. Then the blessings would be upon his head, and not only the blessings actually enjoyed by David, but others promised to him, which neither he nor his successors had been able personally to inherit. Had not David been inspired to sing 'He shall have dominion from one sea to another, from the flood to the world's end.... All kings shall fall down before him, all nations do him service'? Why, the very psalm echoed by the Voice at the Baptism, 'The Lord hath said to me, Thou art my Son,' thus continues: 'Desire of me, and I will give thee the nations for thine inheritance; the uttermost parts of the earth for thy possession.'

We may fairly say that as the first two temptations are hung upon the text 'Thou art my Son,' the third is hung on its immediate sequel, 'The nations thine inheritance.' The inheritance of

Jesus does not lie in the kingdoms of Canaan, but in the king-doms of the world. His mountain-view must be extended by Satan's magic to encompass regions which the eye of Moses could not reach. But, like Moses, he cannot set foot in the pro-mised land. Jesus may proclaim the kingdom of heaven, that is, the world-empire of God in the throne of King Messiah. He can take no direct action to achieve it; he must await the Father's word. And what is cruellest of all, the Kingdom lies away in the future, beyond the barrier of his own death, be-yond the deaths anyhow of most of his contemporaries.

Meanwhile the existing world-powers continued to hold sway, and especially the power of Rome. It was all too clear that the Jew's direct path into the benefits and spoils of a heathen regime ran through the worship of idols. An Israelite could take no part in civic life, could hold no official place however mean, without conforming to heathen custom. The Christians for whom St. Matthew wrote found themselves in the same tantalizing position. The temptation of Jesus was their temptation. The kingdom which was promised to him he had promised to them. For them, as for him, it lay in the mists of the future, or, if clearly seen by the eye of faith, was seen from mountain-tops afar. The heathen world lay close at hand, ready to be entered to-morrow at the cost of compromise. If they would sacrifice to Satan they might have everything; if they would not, they might keep nothing, not even life itself; for by the time St. Matthew wrote a Christian here and there had been given the choice to sacrifice or to die. Whatever diffi-culty moderns may feel over the meaning of Christ's third temptation, St. Matthew's first readers felt none, surely; 'All the kingdoms of the world and the glory of them will I give thee, if thou wilt fall down and worship me' spoke straight to every heart.

They would have found no difficulty either in identifying idolatry with demon-worship. At the time of which we speak, a marked change had come over the Jewish attitude to idolatry. In the classic age of Old Testament religion it had been mocked as the adoration of sticks and stones. The contemporaries of Jesus revived more primitive conceptions: the gods of the heathen were real beings, but they were *tabu*. Only that in Christ's time they were not admitted to be the gods they were taken for. The heathen might suppose themselves to worship spirits who moved the stars and other great parts or elements of nature. They were wrong. Idolatrous cult put them in contact with beings of a baser sort, Satan and his host. Aaron and his fellow tribesmen may have thought that in revering the golden calf they were worshipping the Lord God of Israel himself. They could not have been more grossly mistaken. The spirit who worked the magic, who made the golden calf step ready-made from Aaron's furnace, who licked up the savour of the sacrifice and who inspired the orgy of the worshippers, was no other than the prince of demons. So also when the Christians were invited by idolatrous neighbours to take part in cheerful feasts, it was to Satan's table that they were bidden; it was Satan who held the key to the immediate enjoyment of life, glory, and power in a heathen world.

But however true it is that St. Matthew turns a side-glance on the predicament of his readers, it is of Christ that he writes. Does he really mean to tell us that Christ was tempted to devil-worship? How could he be? The question sounds simple. In fact it is not. Let us take it to pieces. Was Christ *tempted to* devil-worship? Certainly; for that was the thing, and the only thing, Satan suggested he should do. He was not *tempted by* devil-worship, however; he found no attraction in it. He did not envy the worshippers of Jupiter or of Venus their deities.

Still less had he any kinship with those nasty minds that dabble in witchcraft and satanism for the hell of it. At the same time he must have been *tempted by* something. If he had found nothing to attract him in Satan's offer there would have been no temptation at all. The trap was certainly baited; it was not baited with devil-worship, however; it was baited with the riches of the world.

Once again, we have to distinguish. 'All these things will I give thee...' If we take the bait to be the personal monopoly of all material power and glory, Jesus was incapable of being attracted by so monstrous a greed; he might as soon have been attracted by Satanism itself. But we are not obliged to take 'All these things will I give thee' in such a sense. 'All' can mean 'All or any of...' It's all for the asking. Jesus can have what he likes. Taken in this sense, the offer contains many items which cannot fail to attract a healthy mind. It is sheer morbidity to have no taste for freedom from hunger, thirst, and cold; for any single charm or elegance of civilized life; for physical means to carry out good purposes, or to be the benefactor of others; for a position of influence to sway the counsels of mankind. Such things are good to have, could they be had on decent terms. Any of them may be refused for any of several reasons. They would distract us from the pursuit of more important aims; they would place us in a position of advantage over others which we prefer to forgo; they can only be had by employing detestable means. But from whatever motive they are refused, they are in themselves attractive to a healthy mind, and the refusal of them costs us a natural regret.

So Jesus is *tempted by* much of what Satan offers. Now no one is tempted by any object or any prospect who has no practicable means of attaining it. If I told you I was tempted by a summer holiday on the back of the moon what would you an-

swer? If you wished to be polite, you would say 'How delight-
ful! I had no idea that space-travel was so far advanced.' For
you would have to pretend to suppose some possible means of
my doing what I say tempts me. You would secretly think I had
gone off my head, or I would not be entertaining the possibility
of what is not yet practicable. If I said I was tempted by a summer in Japan you would entertain no such suspicion. But you
would think to yourself 'Why does he say *tempted?* I suppose
he is in moral doubt whether the time could be spared, or the
money. His being *tempted by* Japan means that he is *tempted to*
borrow money from the bank.' It would be inadventurous or
narrow-minded not to be *tempted by* the Japanese holiday; it
might be irresponsible, or downright immoral, to run so far
into the red. The point can probably be settled quickly by cast-
ing up my accounts and reviewing my sources of income. Until
I have had opportunity to do so, no one thinks the worse of me
for playing with the temptation. Once I have seen that the
means required are such as cannot be justified, I am to be
blamed if I delay to turn my back on the tempting idea.

So, if there is any temptation, Christ must be *tempted by*
what is offered him, and must think that there is some means
of his getting it. His belief in the means need go no further
than supposing that the person offering can make his offer
good. But once the means or conditions for taking up the offer
are made clear he rejects it; on those terms, no! 'Depart from
me, Satan, for it is written, The Lord thy God shalt thou worship and him only serve.'

In what I have just said I have for simplicity's sake taken
the story as it stands. In fact we must say about the third temptation what we said about the second—it has the mythical or
symbolical character of a vision or even of a dream. 'Go to
God's house and jump off the roof' is a parable of what 'tempt-

ing God' is like; it is not an action to which we should be tempted in waking life; yet in the vision parable is reality. 'Worshipping Satan to gain the world' is similarly a temptation which ceaselessly besets the servants of God. It does not take the legendary form of all royalty and all riches offered in exchange for an act of physical homage to a Satan with horns and hoofs. Yet it is in this form that Christ encounters it; and why? he encounters it in vision.

Fortunately for us St. Matthew does not leave us long in doubt how the third temptation should be practically interpreted. The Sermon on the Mount follows as close upon the Temptations as it can conveniently be made to do. We shall presently observe how widely and how deeply the Sermon reflects the lessons which the Temptations bring to light. We do not wish to anticipate in any detail here what we shall have to say then. But while we are about it we wish to justify the interpretation we have made of Satan's offer. Perhaps the following few quotations will speak for themselves.

Heap not to yourselves treasures upon earth...but heap to yourselves treasures in heaven.... For where your treasure is your heart will be.... No man can serve two masters.... Ye cannot serve God and Mammon.... Consider the lilies.... Solomon in all his glory was not arrayed like one of these.... Be not concerned to say What shall we eat...drink...or wear? For after all these things do the heathen seek; whereas your Father knoweth that ye need all these things. Seek first his kingdom and his righteousness; so all these things will be given you besides.

One can hardly read such words, coming where they do, without hearing an echo of the choice which the last temptation so dramatically poses. We cannot serve two masters—not Satan and the Father of Jesus, not the God of Israel and the golden calf. Solomon had the kingdom and the glory; there is no need to envy him when we look at the flower of the field. God clothes the grass, and he will clothe us. Dress, food and drink are our essential needs. If we seek his kingdom we are assured of them, if not in this age, then in the Age to Come.

CHAPTER VI

■ ■ ■

'Son of God'

W HATEVER WE MAY say of the third temptation, the first two are openly concerned with Christ's standing as Son of God. The meaning and the very fact of his sonship are challenged by Satan. We have already considered in general how it was possible for Christ to feel the force of Satan's attack. We have discussed the paradox involved in his incarnate state: as man on earth, the Son of God must find his way into being what he eternally is. For him, as for each one of us, it was the work of a lifetime to realize his own being. He was one of us in having that task to perform; he differed from us in truly accomplishing it. He differed from us even more radically in having a deeper and more mysterious being to realize. We hardly get round to living as God's creatures; it was for him to live as God's only Son. And, as we were saying, his living himself into being God's Son meant his thinking himself into being it. The tradition of his people supplied no ready-made ideas adequate to the mental task. It was for Jesus to revalue an old coinage and spell new truths with ancient characters.

St. Matthew means seriously to tell us that Christ's call to his ministry called him to the understanding of his Sonship. He makes no pretence of uncovering for us the actual working of Christ's mind on this question at the time of his temptation. He does claim to tell us how he repelled the tempter; but not how he put together the conception of Sonship to God. Yet the evangelist has his own way of hinting at the materials available to Christ and at the way they took shape in his mind. As a student of the Old Testament he can show us what was there for Christ to use, and what use (to judge by his subsequent words and actions) he came to make of it. In what field of ideas, then, does the evangelist see Christ to move when he begins to understand himself as Son to God?

St. Matthew builds up stone by stone the edifice of Christ's divine claim beginning from the first word of his book. He starts by saying of Jesus no more than that he is Messiah, and therefore of course son of David, and if of David, then of Abraham. No Jew could claim less for any one whom he honoured with the messianic title. St. Matthew proceeds to fill out the genealogy from Abraham through David down to Jesus. In doing so he makes two points. While the line of fathers is legally correct there were several irregular mothers. Judah, the father of the messianic tribe, got his heir through a sort of incest with his daughter-in-law. David himself got his heir through a regularized adultery. David's grandmother was no daughter of Israel but a Moabitess; his great-grandmother was a harlot from heathen Jericho. Divine providence, it appears, had taken small account of legitimacy or of propriety in giving heirs to the messianic line; and so we are prepared for the supreme paradox—the heir to all the promises has not a drop of Davidic blood in his veins but is grafted into the stock by miracle. The bride whom Joseph takes to wife is with child already, though by no earthly parent. The look of the matter is scandalous, the truth of it divine.

The second point in St. Matthew's transcript of the genealogy is this: it falls into three equal blocks of generations, each block a double seven: from Abraham to David, from David to exile in Babylon, from exile to Jesus. If we look at the genealogy in relation to the messianic title, what are we to make of its three-part division? Are not we to consider that Christ inherits the promise made to Abraham, under which the people of God lived until the time of David, and indeed continue to live; only that with the coming of David a new promise was added, a promise restricted to David's family? It had a visible fulfilment in the period of the monarchy, when David continued to reign through his successors. Then, with the exile, a period began in which the Davidic line went underground and hope was set on a coming Messiah, that is, on Jesus. In short, there were the generations of Abraham, the generations of David, and the generations leading to Messiah.

In the first verse of his book St. Matthew writes the three names in the backwards order, Jesus, David, Abraham. In filling out the genealogy he comes forward again from Abraham through David to Jesus. His next move is to turn over from listing to narrative. In 1:18 he places himself at the moment of Christ's nativity, and from that point delves back into the history again. The angel who appears to Joseph reminds him that he is the son of David, and encourages him to take his wife, though she is pregnant. Was not David's great-grandmother a harlot from Jericho? Was not his grandmother an alien, wooed in a field and bedded on a threshing-floor? Did not David beget his own heir on the wife of Uriah the Hittite, already pregnant at the time of her official marriage? St. Matthew quotes in support an oracle from the days of David's dynasty, 'The virgin shall conceive.' The Magi follow on to prove that a King of Israel must spring from David's city, Bethlehem; a son of David, not the upstart Herod, is God's king in Jewry. Their sign is a miraculous star; for had not Balaam's famous prophecy joined with the rising of a star the dawn of David's empire?

With the flight of the Holy Family to Egypt and the massacre of innocents we delve back farther into the history behind Jesus. What happens to him now recalls the generations before David, when Abraham's race went down into Egypt, when Pharaoh massacred their infant sons and when Moses was (like Jesus) wonderfully preserved. Those were the days of exodus, when Israel wandered through barren lands, as Abraham and Jacob had done before them. And the next act of St. Matthew's drama is in the wilderness. There it is that John preaches and, in his preaching, goes to the root of the genealogy. Let not the offspring of vipers say to themselves 'We have Abraham for father'; God can raise children to Abraham from the very stones. What is the worth of legitimate descent? Was not the fourth from Abraham, Judah's heir, a fruit of incest? If St. John's hearers are to merit divine election they must repent; they must receive *the* elected heir, the prince who comes baptizing with the Holy Ghost.

So the Baptist, with his wilderness-setting and his Abraham sermon, recalls the first period of the genealogy; and Christ places himself in the same setting when he first comes to John, and afterwards departs into the wilderness alone. As to what happens when he is there, we have no need to repeat what we wrote in our first chapter. We showed how strongly and how clearly Christ's Baptism and subsequent Temptations reproduce the pattern of Israel's exodus from Egypt and sojourn in the wilderness.

Before we go further, let us pause and recall the simple repetition of themes which we have so far noted.

1 The title: Jesus, son of David, son of Abraham.

2 The genealogy: Abraham and thirteen descents, David and thirteen descents, thirteen more descents to Jesus.

3 The history: The birth of Jesus recalls the days of David, his infancy, the times after Abraham: so does the Baptist's mission and Christ's association with it.

It may be that in the passages we have just schematized St. Matthew has got all he wants out of a to-and-fro movement over the three names and the three historical eras attached to them. Or perhaps not. He has gone backwards in the title and come forward again in the genealogy; he has gone back once more in the story of Jesus; will he not come forward again there too? Surely he will; surely, indeed, he has done so. Only look at the three scenes of the temptation.

In literal fact all three temptations happen in the wilderness, and even symbolically viewed, all three represent temptations besetting Israel in that wilderness-time; all three, accordingly, are rejected by Christ in quotations from the wilderness story of Deuteronomy. Yet there is another side to the matter. Beside the real scene of the temptations we have the visionary settings. Only the first trial is unambiguously cited in the wilderness. The second is at the Temple in David's capital city, that Temple which David planned and left Solomon to build. As for the form of the temptation itself, it does not derive from the Exodus story. Christ is to tempt God, but not as Israel there did, by challenging him to give water in a waterless place. No, he is to tempt his Father by the dramatic invocation of a promise given to David in one of David's psalms. With the third temptation the setting changes again. It is as far from the scene of former Jewish royal power as it is from Christ's retreat in the Judaean wilderness. It is an imaginary mountain height affording a view over all the kingdoms of the world. And these kingdoms are evidently seen as heathen; the gate of entry into them is compromise with idolatry. The faithful Israelite is excluded and views them from without. Once again, though the temptation to idolatry had beset Israel in the wilderness days and also in monarchical times, the particular form it here takes is characteristic of the third period in St. Matthew's genealogy, the days after the exile. In the days of subjection to the mighty kingdoms of the heathen, the Jew met the challenge 'Fall down and worship, or you will be shut out. Worship, and we admit you to power and riches.' Such is the situation under Nebuchadnezzar and Darius according to the Book of Daniel, or under Greco-Syrian tyranny according to the Books of Maccabees. Since every one knows the narratives in Daniel, it may be of more interest to recall the Maccabees. 'The king's officers said to Mattathias, Thou art a ruler great and honourable in this city, with sons and brethren to strengthen thee. Come thou first and do the king's commandment (of idol sacrifice).... So thou and thy sons shall be among the King's Friends; ye shall be honoured with silver and gold and gifts in abundance.'

It was the favourite thought of Christian writers from the end of the second century A.D., that Jesus Christ had summed up in his incarnate action the past of the human race, and lived straight the life which so many generations had lived crooked. These writers laid chief stress on Christ's reversal of Adam's legendary disobedience. St. Matthew thinks less of Adam than of the chosen people; of how they had erred since first their stock was taken into God's special service through the call of Abraham. So in three scenes he shows how Christ met the temptations attaching to the three phases of Israel's history: the phase of nomadic life after Abraham, the phase of established monarchy after David, and the phase of subjection to heathen empire after exile in Babylon. The nomad is in the desert, and his typical temptation is concerned with the bare necessities of life. The monarchical establishment is in the royal city crowned by Solomon's Temple; and its temptation is presumption, an unjustified reliance on divine aid. How constantly the great prophets of the monarchy did scourge that sin! The Jewish subject of Nebuchadnezzar, of Antiochus or of Caesar is watching the panorama of empire; and his temptation is apostasy, or at least compromise with Satan.

So Christ's temptations strike root into the historic past. There is nothing artificial about that, for the past is still with him, as it is with all of us. Civilization has overlaid the nomad's anxiety for bare subsistence with layers of more sophisticated concern; but the care for subsistence remains. Jesus in his day had not far to walk into the wilderness before he felt the pinch; he might feel it in a bad season though he stayed at home. It was not for nothing that he taught his Galileans to pray, 'Give us this day our daily bread.' And if Jacob's hunger was with them still, so was David's glamour. Though David's throne had fallen, the Jews' pride in the Temple and trust in privilege remained, if, indeed, it was not actually intensified; witness the blind folly which led them to rebellion against Rome and their city's downfall in A.D. 70. As to the third temptation, it needs no words to show that it beset them still. Was not Jesus living in 'the times of the Gentiles,' and looking over pagan hedges into an orchard of forbidden fruit?

Before we go further with the summing up of the past in Christ's temptation, let us pause to notice a point of St. Matthew's style. His running to and fro over the three names with their three associated eras began, as we saw, from a single line, 'The genealogy of Jesus Christ, son of David, son of Abraham.' He finishes off the to-and-fro movement with a line equally short. After exhibiting temptations concerned with (a) the satisfaction of need, (b) the reliance on angels and (c) the dismissal of Satan, St. Matthew reverses the sequence once more. 'Then (c) the devil leaveth him and (b) lo, angels approached and (a) ministered to his need.' How conscious St. Matthew's shaping of his work was, we cannot tell; he may have done it by a sort of instinct. But whether it was instinct or whether it was art, here is the pattern into which it falls:

1: 1, summary: c, b, a.

1: 2-27, short passage: a, b, c.

1: 18-3: 17, long passage: c, b, a.

4: 1-10, short passage: a, b, c.

4: 11, summary: c, b, a.

My readers will not want to dwell further on the formal balance of St. Matthew's style. Let us return to the materials which Israel's history offered Jesus towards a picture of divine sonship. We may begin by taking up once more the voice from heaven which sounded at his baptism. We have observed that it wakes the echo of three scriptural texts particularly:

Thou art my son, this day have I fathered thee (Ps. 2).

Thy son, thine only beloved (Genesis 22).

My servant in whom I am well pleased; I have put my Spirit upon him (Isaiah 42).

Of these three texts the first alone is strictly messianic. Its application to our Saviour proclaims him David's heir; he has that special Sonship to God which is the king's prerogative; a sonship which the Judaean dynasty held in no more than a formal sense, by virtue of their royal office, but of which Messiah would realize the spirit and the power. The second text looks in a different direction. It makes Christ be to God what Isaac was to Abraham, a son only beloved. As the text stands, it does not in strict logic relate Christ to Abraham at all; it makes him God's Isaac, not Abraham's. But logic or no logic, it is difficult to avoid feeling the force of the suggestion that God's Isaac is the true Isaac, heir of the promises God gave to Abraham and to his seed. The suggestion is confirmed by the third text. For any one who reads Isaiah 41-42 continuously must see that 'the servant in whom God is well-pleased' is (if not Isaac) Isaac's heir, Jacob or Israel; the old Greek version says so in so many words; and St. Matthew was acquainted with that version. Now the whole divine promise descending from Abraham to Isaac descended on from Isaac to his sole spiritual inheritor, Jacob or Israel. To be Israel or Jacob meant spiritually to be what Isaac was—that is, hander down of the promises and sole ancestor of the people of God.

So one of the three texts echoed by the baptism-voice is messianic or Davidic; the other two point through the figure of Isaac to that of Israel. Now there can be no doubt that in orthodox Jewish thought Israel's sonship to God was primary, Messiah's secondary. 'Israel is my son, my firstborn' said the divine voice to Pharaoh; and if it was later said of David's son 'I will make him my firstborn, higher than the kings of the earth' it was because Israel's pre-eminence could only be achieved in the pre-eminent power of his king. Israel was God's son corporately; Messiah would be God's son representatively.

In saying that Israel had the sonship corporately we have allowed our thought to slide from Israel the patriarch, commonly called Jacob, to Israel the nation, otherwise called Children of Israel, who were rescued from Egypt and installed in Canaan. Never mind, for in so sliding between the two we are only doing what our biblical writers have done on every other page.

In their minds the last single ancestor of the whole chosen people was felt to be present in his descendants, their fortunes and their privileges were his. We cannot perhaps ever quite say that any scriptural text uses 'Israel' as a simple collective noun, naming a multitude. Some shadow of Father Jacob's person clings to the word and gives unity to the idea.

So 'Israel' is an individual person, sliding over into a collective person; and the collective aspect is unmistakable in the third of the texts we have just listed. 'Israel, the Lord's Servant,' of whom Isaiah speaks may be Jacob the patriarch in certain passages, where it is God's choice of him that is in the prophet's mind. But when his subject is the destiny Israel was chosen to fulfil, he must be taken to speak of the people descended from Jacob. For the patriarch of that name did not execute in his own person his God-given commission. Was the Jacob of Genesis a light to the Gentiles or the ultimate prince of the world? He could only claim such titles through his remote descendants, and on the score of what they were destined to do.

The oddity of the Jewish mind in sliding between the idea of a common ancestor and the idea of a people descended from him, would be in itself no more than a historical curiosity. What interests us is its serviceableness to Christ. For it provided an adaptable image through which he could picture his own representative function. King Messiah, son of David, is Son of God—not because kings are divine beings, a race apart, the representatives of heaven enthroned on the necks of earthly subjects. No; Messiah is Son of God because Israel is God's elected son and Messiah makes Israel's sonship a reality. He is in spiritual fact what Israel was in name; and the people of God realize their corporate sonship to their Lord by association with his Anointed.

The collective aspect of Israel's sonship, and its bearing on the call of Christ, is emphasized by the whole setting of the temptation-story. In answering Satan Christ places himself under the law addressed through Moses to the people of God. He takes to himself the 'thou' of Moses's Deuteronomic discourse, a 'thou' which designates the collective Israel. 'Hear, O Israel...*thou* shalt love the Lord thy God' gives us the form. It is in the same sense that we have to read the passages to which Jesus refers: 'That *thou* mightest learn that man shall not live by bread alone....As a father would discipline his son, the Lord thy God disciplines *thee*'—'*Thou* shalt not tempt the Lord thy God'—'The Lord thy God shalt *thou* worship...' Israel is the son whom God disciplines, Israel of whom God said to Pharaoh 'He is my son, my firstborn: let my son go, that he may serve me.' The text is in Exodus 4. St. Matthew does not quote it, for it scarcely fits his story. He cites instead the equivalent text from Hosea: 'I have called my son out of Egypt.'

Probably most readers of Deuteronomy take the 'thou' which sprinkles its pages as an address to any Israelite, much as they would take the 'you' which appeals to them from the advertisement hoardings: 'Try delicious...s; *you* will simply love them.' And there are many Deuteronomic passages in which such an interpretation is reasonable enough. For time and again Moses lays down Israel's duty in the particular case, as it affects (let us say) any responsible householder. But the duty is Israel's duty; and the collective aspect of the 'thou' is emphasized in St. Matthew's Deuteronomic quotations, by being set in parallel with the title 'Son of God.' For 'Son of God' was the title of Israel, not of any Israelite in his private capacity. 'If thou art the Son of God, cast thyself down...'—

'No, for it is written, Thou (Son of God, thou Israel) shalt not tempt the Lord thy God.'

It is perhaps worth remarking that it is Satan who appeals to a strictly messianic text: David, or David's anointed offspring, so he claims, is entitled to throw himself upon the air, and on angelic intervention. Christ makes his appeal throughout to words of God addressing the son whom he brought up out of Egypt, his firstborn Israel.

There is no need for us to admire every trick of biblical speech. The double-edged use of the name 'Israel' was picturesque, it stirred national feeling, it awakened historical or legendary echoes. It did not assist clarity of thought, for no one knew what was meant by the presence of a patriarch in his descendants, nor (conversely) by the crediting to him of their sufferings and achievements. The ancient Israelite was anything rather than an exact philosopher. He was impressed, no doubt, as more sophisticated minds have been, by the phenomenon of group consciousness. In certain circumstances and in certain aspects of its common life a people feels itself to have a single soul and to form a single body or person. It is (said the ancient Israelite) as though his living children had crept back into the loins of the patriarch from whom they had their common origin. If they feel common interest and find themselves in common action, is it not because his blood runs in all their veins, because they are all Israel?

Such thinking, or picturing rather, was a piece of primitive barbarism. As theory it was grossly mythical; as a practical approach to nationhood it was as double-edged as other patriotic fictions—cohesive and inspiring, but cramping and dangerous. Whatever we read the Bible for, we do not read it for the purpose of barbarizing our social theory. And even if we did wish to borrow this particular image, we could not. Neither the English nor any other modern people has a reputed common ancestor on whom to pin the patriarchal part. Late medieval romance somewhat halfheartedly invented a hero called Brut, who had given the British race a being and a name. The invention never caught on; and it is certainly too late now to blow it into a flame. We cannot talk of creeping back into King Brut's loins, even when we are talking national heroics.

The ambivalent idea of Israel served its turn. We are not called upon to justify it. Indeed it has gone so far down the river of time that it excites neither our blame nor our commendation. What does move us is the art of God's providence, which placed such a mental tool ready to the hand of Jesus. For what was unintelligible in relation to Jacob became truth and clarity in relation to him.

The piece missing from the old pattern was any real link, any actual communion between the people and their long-buried patriarch. Whereas Messiah was to be an everlasting king; by being Son to God and living it out, by associating others at the same time with himself, he could bring a new Israel into sonship with God, and he could keep them in it. When Christ began his ministry it was still a mystery how he was to remain in real and personal communion with ever increasing multitudes. By the time St. Matthew wrote, the mystery had cleared; divine wisdom had found a way. We need not suppose that Jesus in the wilderness had probed the mysterious 'how.' It is safest to assume in his mind the scheme of belief common to his day. The enthronement of Messiah in power and glory would involve a transformation of the world. Would it not be such as to allow of real fellowship between Messiah and his brethren? Meanwhile it was for him to be what he was, Son of God, and to associate others with him as occasion offered. Was not his first recorded act after he returned from the wilderness a calling of four disciples?

However heart-warming to Israelites was the thought of their identity with their patriarch, it could not provide the real basis of their unity. The intention to be true children of Jacob provided no programme of common life—not, that is, if you stuck to what the legendary or historical figure of Jacob could give you. You could make the Jew's duty a call to be the true child of Israel if you liked, but you smuggled in under the name all manner of rules and obligations which had nothing to do with Father Jacob. A true son of Israel keeps the Law of Moses; the patriarch Israel did not; the Law was not given until centuries after his death. A true son of Israel supports the Levitical priesthood and pays dues to the Temple. Not so Jacob, there were no Levites in his day and no temple either. The religion of Israel was not Jacobism; the faith of the Church is Christianity. Because Christ is the life of the Church, no rules or institutions are justified in Christendom but those which make union with Christ effectual. If Israel was not held together by the cage of Moses's rules, what unity could it have? The only unity Jacob could give it was the bond of common descent, the solidarity of a blood-group. Christ, the new Israel, could be a light to the Gentiles because spiritual union with him was an open possibility. You could be related to Jacob by physical relation only, by membership in his tribe; or at the most, by the fiction of adoption into it.

The temptation-story is not the whole Gospel. It is unreasonable to complain at the absence from so short a passage of some single darling truth. We can look for what we miss on other pages. But when we have digested so sensible a piece of advice, we may still feel a certain disquiet. The temptation story is to be typical both of Christ's temptations and of ours.

How is it, then, that the issue of charity to mankind does not make itself felt? Two-thirds of our temptations, and those which our consciences take most seriously, are concerned either with the neglect of others' claims, or the preferring of our own. What should we think of it if a Christian made a confession without a single reference to his fellowmen, but wholly concerned with his relation to his Creator, with the pursuit of his calling, and with the control of his appetites? Should not we say that such a conscience, however tender, was alarmingly self-centered? And is it not disappointing that our Lord's temptations take place in a wilderness of spiritual solitude? That obedience to God and rejection of worldliness are their sole concern?

What shall we say to this? First of all we shall be bound to insist on the obvious point, that Christ's temptation arises from his situation; that is, out of his call to be Messiah and Son of God. No doubt daily life at Nazareth had its temptations, bearing on other members of the household, on customers and townsfolk. But for the while Christ's face is set in another direction and these matters are behind his back. Then in the second place we shall urge the corporate connections of that Sonship on which Christ takes his stand. He rejects a Sonship of privilege for a Sonship of humble obedience; and in so doing he puts himself under the law of religion which binds his brethren. If he aspires to be a new Israel, it is by first being a humble Israelite. It is undeniable that his temptation concerns his relation with his God and Father; but the Satanic falsification of this relation is precisely one which would destroy his solidarity with those he comes to save.

In conclusion let us look back at the beginning of the Gospel we are studying. St. Luke perhaps introduces Jesus as the child who had a divine but not a human father; St. Matthew does not. He introduces him as the promised heir of David and of Abraham. In writing out the genealogy he notes the part divine election played in the succession of heirs—it was not always the child with the purest blood or the highest legitimate claims who carried on the line. And so he comes to the final step, at which divine initiative simply grafted in the ultimate inheritor of the promises. St. Matthew teaches a paradoxical doctrine: neither Abraham nor David, whether in himself or through his descendants, could beget *the* son of David or *the* son of Abraham. Only the sheer action of the Holy Ghost could give the patriarchs the son capable of inheriting a blessedness covenanted to their seed. Israel collectively and David's heir representatively had been called firstborn son of God; neither could actualize the sonship imputed to him apart from the Spirit's generative power at work in Mary.

The Church came to think, and rightly to think, of God the Son coming as it were to earth from heaven and putting on a coat of flesh in Mary's womb. But Jesus had to think his way into the understanding of himself and of his calling. We need not suppose that he started from the point which the faith of the Church ultimately reached. He would more naturally begin by deepening the messianic hopes current in Israel. Even supposing what St. Matthew surely means us to suppose, that Jesus had been told the secret of his birth, what would be more natural than for him to interpret the fact along the lines his evangelist suggests? Divine miracle had given to the house of David and of Abraham *the* son in whom their sonship to God might be realized.

The evangelist suggests it, he does not state it. He does not dare to tell us what he could scarcely claim to know—how Jesus in the solitude of the desert thought of his sonship to God. He simply piles together Old Testament materials on which it is very reasonable to suppose Jesus went to work; materials which, indeed, form the natural background to Christ's baptism as St. Mark had already narrated it before St. Matthew wrote.

CHAPTER VII

■ ■ ■

The Sequel

T HE AIM OF this chapter will be to show how Christ's subsequent teaching gives expression to his three victories
over Satan. So that we may not lose the thread, we will begin
by following the evangelist's story on from the point we have
reached. It was on hearing the report of John Baptist's arrest,
he says, that Jesus put an end to his period of retirement; as
though John's arrest were a signal he was waiting for. The
temptations had carried a lesson, but it was not a lesson of
detailed or positive guidance. The Son of God was to be loyal
and patient; he was not to force the Father's hand. There was
no program of action here, such as he could set about to fulfil.
How different was the call to take up the Baptist's burden
where John laid it down! It challenged action forthwith. St.
Matthew shows us Jesus simply going on where John left off.
His message is initially the same message, word for word: 'Repent, for the kingdom of heaven is at hand.'

The period of withdrawal was over, and Jesus exchanged the
desert for the town. But he did not surrender the detachment he
had achieved. He left home, family and business; he migrated
from Nazareth to the center of Jewish Galilee, Capernaum. Not
that he set up house even there. He could lodge with Peter's
family in the place, but no home any longer was his: 'The Son
of Man had not where to lay his head,' except in so far as he
was hospitably received; and he frequently withdrew by choice
into uninhabited country.

His first recorded action was to call four companions likewise from their trade and family, associating them with his vagrant life. Thus accompanied, he toured Galilee, healing and preaching, often from the pulpits of the sabbath synagogues. His work and especially his healings collected a mass of people from all over Palestine. In face of the assembling multitude Jesus withdrew into the mountains, to equip (it would seem) his disciples with the knowledge they needed, if ever they were to instruct such crowds. So they went into the mountain as Moses went up Sinai, and received the living oracles of the Lord.

Christ's instruction for his disciples began with the Beatitudes. He blessed that condition into which he had called them, and in which he had first placed himself, by the stand he took in the wilderness. The blessings are given in general form, to fall on the heads of any who deserve them: 'Blessed are those who...' But the last blessing is no sooner delivered, than it is applied to the disciples: 'Blessed are the persecuted.... Blessed are ye, when man shall persecute you.'

The Beatitudes, as they proceed, bring other themes into play, but they take their start from where the temptations end. 'Blessed are the poor in spirit.' 'In spirit' is not easy to translate. But for the misleading suggestion of asceticism, we might render 'the poor by choice.' The poor of whom Christ speaks accept poverty, not because it is good to be in want, but because plenty is not to be had without either greed or compromise. It is because they are set against such evils that they are happy to be poor. A man might be poor, who coveted the kingdoms of the ungodly world, so long as he coveted them in vain; he would not be poor in spirit, though. Christ is poor in spirit, for he refuses Satan's offer when it is made him.

The promise given to the spiritual poor links Christ's last temptation with the message he caught up from the lips of the Baptist. He who had renounced 'the kingdoms of the world and all their glory' found himself heralding the kingdom of heaven; that is to say, the establishment of God's empire over his earthly subjects. When heaven reigned, Jesus was to be the visible king, in virtue of a Sonship to God which his temptations had tested. More in particular, he was fitted to reign for God by refusing to reign with Satan; by being 'poor in spirit,' by purifying his heart of all hankering after Satanic wealth or power. His disciples, in virtue of the same renunciation, are fit partakers of his royalty—for when the poor are promised the kingdom, they are made princes, not subjects. By unity of heart with the royal will, they share the sovereignty of heaven over earth.

The second Beatitude develops the idea. It speaks of consolation. Now 'the consolation of Israel' was a standing equivalent for redemption to come. This consolation, says Christ, is reserved for those whom nothing else will console; who do not fool themselves with substitute satisfactions, nor make a paganized world their home. They mourn for the Satanic tyranny under which Israel groans; and they mourn the sins of Israel, which have brought such a punishment.

The third Beatitude chimes with the first. 'They shall inherit the earth,' echoes 'The kingdom of heaven is theirs.' The English suggests a contrast where the Greek states a parallel. Christ's first hearers would not have imagined the poor as staking out a claim somewhere above the stars, while the meek received their portion on the earth's surface. In their view, when the kingdom of heaven came, it would come to rule the earth. The poor would be princes and the meek landholders in that empire.

The beatitude on the meek is a psalm-quotation. The most obvious reason for its presence among the Beatitudes is the need to combat what was called Zealotry. The Zealots were revolutionaries of the violent sort. They were as uncompromising as any one could wish in rejecting Satan's kingdom with all its works; but they held that loyalty to the divine kingdom meant rebellion against Caesar. Christ ranges himself for once with Pharisaic orthodoxy when he insists upon the psalmist's paradox: those who inherit the land will be those who do not force their claims. But however topical the anti-Zealot bearing of the beatitude may be, its relation to Christ's temptation is equally plain. The Son of God does not take the law into his own hands. He will not even bid the stones be bread for him; still less will he dictate to the providence of God by violent action.

The fourth Beatitude takes us right back into the wilderness situation. 'He fasted forty days and forty nights,...and...said, Man shall not live by bread alone...' 'Blessed are they that hunger and thirst after righteousness.' 'After righteousness'— the phrase is not to be taken as allegorizing away the hunger and thirst. The blessing is not meant for those who, hungry for justice, eat their three square meals a day. To understand the language used, we must begin by recalling that fasting with the Jews was a form of supplication; you were throwing yourself on the divine mercy. What you hungered for, if your fast was sincere, was not so much the food of which you willingly deprived yourself, as the boon you craved from God; it might be forgiveness, it might be victory or deliverance. Later in the Sermon we shall find Jesus commenting on voluntary fasting, in conjunction with prayer. He takes it for granted that a sincere fast obtains a man the favour of heaven. Otherwise why should he trouble to warn fasting souls against loss of heavenly credit by indulgence of worldly motives? A man who fasts sincerely may 'hunger and thirst after righteousness,' but he will fast all the same, and hunger for bread.

It is not clear, however, that the 'hunger and thirst' of the Beatitude is voluntary fasting. The poor, who are the first subjects of Christ's blessing, go hungry, but scarcely from choice. If they choose hunger, they only do so in choosing poverty; and poverty they do not so much choose, as accept, because they will not lose their souls to gain the world. They ask for no relief of their condition but that which 'righteousness' will bring; and 'righteousness' means the establishment of God's will. God's ears are specially open to the cry of the poor; those whose hope is wholly set upon God are powerful intercessors; their enforced want has the value of a meritorious fast.

The fourth Beatitude falls upon the merciful. To judge from the sequel, the mercy principally blessed is that active compassion which relieves distress. 'Mercy' is the biblical Greek for 'charity' or almsgiving. As the third Beatitude blesses those who lack what they need, the fourth blesses those who give away what they have. Almsgiving and fasting, with prayer, were the typical acts of merit in the Jewish religion. Jesus returns to them later in the Sermon. Fasting and prayer have a direct relation to Christ's temptations, almsgiving has none. From this point onwards the Beatitudes develop independently of the Temptations, and it does not concern us to follow them further.

The Beatitudes swing away in the direction of other themes, but that does not mean there will be no more reflection on the Temptations in the Sermon on the Mount. We have already witnessed the boomerang flight of St. Matthew's thought; how he loves to reverse direction and come back over the course he has covered. The Sermon on the Mount is no exception. No sooner are the eight Beatitudes complete, than the Speaker begins to come back over the ground which they have marked out. The last blessing of the eight applies, he says, to his disciples; they will be privileged to undergo persecution for righteousness, in fellowship with the Lord's prophets. For they too in their day are the salt of the earth, and light of the world; so long, that is, as their deeds answer to their professions. No error could be more gross, says Christ, than the idea that he has come to take away the rule of good deeds. The rule is in the Law of God, and he has come to give it its fullest force.

Jesus proceeds to take examples of legal rules to show how they can be kept in the spirit as well as in the letter. In the course of discussing them, he takes occasion to reflect upon the seventh Beatitude, and then the sixth, so continuing his retracing of the ground. It is not enough, he says, to abstain from murder; the disciple must be an active peacemaker. Nor is it enough to avoid the act of adultery; we must shun the adultery of the mind. 'Blessed are the pure in heart' the sixth Beatitude had said 'for they shall see God': and the seventh 'Blessed are the peacemakers, for they shall be called the sons of God.'

Jesus continues through several more cases of legal prohibition, showing how they can move us to active goodness. He turns next to the acknowledged good works of Judaism, almsgiving, prayer and fasting. Thus he returns to the fifth and fourth Beatitudes, with their blessings on charity, and on hunger after righteousness. And so we come back to that part of the Beatitudes which concerns us; for it is the first four that so plainly reflect the Temptations in the wilderness.

The Lord's Sermon shows a change of method at this point. The last four Beatitudes have been touched on in reversed order, one by one. The first four are taken in the lump. There is nothing which should surprise us in that. For these four Beatitudes are much closer to one another than those that follow them in the list. Poverty, mourning and hunger are all forms of distress, and the promise given to them is in each case the corresponding opposite. Meekness is not a deprivation, but it is the virtue most admirable in the deprived. Then secondly, we have to notice that the Sermon is concerned with conduct. Now poverty, mourning and hunger are not duties. They are conditions of life which, when combined with faith, throw men on the compassion of God. The only duty in which they find a natural place is the duty of prayer. The Sermon, as we have seen, treats almsgiving, prayer and fasting together. Almsgiving, through its Jewish name of 'mercy,' recalls the fifth Beatitude. Prayer brings in the preceding four.

The Lord's Prayer is well known to be largely a rephrasing of clauses picked from the current Jewish form. But the choice, wording and arrangement can still be such as to echo the Beatitudes. He who prays is a beggarman, asking for what Christ's blessing promised to beggars—the kingdom of (our Father in) heaven; a hungry man, asking for daily bread; a mournful, penitent man, asking forgiveness of his sins; a meek man and a gentle, who, by not exacting his rights from his neighbours, merits the remission of his debt to heaven.

The Prayer gains still further in depth of meaning by being placed on the background of Christ's temptations. The beggary which dares pray for the kingdom to come is a beggary which beggars itself, refusing the kingdoms of the world and all their splendours. Such is the prayer which Jesus prays with the whole force of his sacrificial life, and which we are privileged to pray with him. And when we ask for daily bread, it is in union with this Son who thought it arrogance to bid the stones be loaves, and trusted the Father by whose every word a man may live.

Here are remarkable enrichments to the Prayer; but it is the beginning and the end of it which gain most from the wilderness-narrative. 'Father..., hallowed be thy name.' The whole temptation turned upon Sonship, and how it stands related to the Father in heaven. What else was Christ concerned for in any assault of Satan, but to hallow and reverence a Father's name? 'Lead us not into temptation, but deliver us from the Wicked One.' Is it not characteristic of Christ's simplicity, of his humanness, that he lets us pray against what recent experience reminded him we must often undergo? We pray to be spared the hour of trial, and not to be left in the hands of the tempter's malice. For prayer is the expression of the heart, the voice of nature. We must pray for whatever is normally good, health, food, peace of soul. We do right to desire such things for others as for ourselves, and to make our desire known to God. We know that we may be denied such benefits, and that a higher will than ours may turn the denial to our profit.

The Lord's Prayer finds its place in the discussion of the three works of merit, almsgiving, prayer and fasting. After treating them in order one by one, the divine teacher continues in a less formal style, drawing the three themes together. Charity is his dominant topic—charity or, as it was commonly called in those days, the frank, or simple, eye. (Notice, and you will see that a man set to refuse a beggar screws up his eyes; the open, unfolded eye welcomes a request.) If fasting is still under consideration in this part of the Sermon, it is not so much the formal practice as the spirit of it—a detachment from concern with our own provision, such that we are able to give freely in relief of others. As for prayer, it is undisguisedly viewed as petition for blessings. The God who forgives the forgiving will give to the giving, says Christ. So do for others all you would have God do for you; that is the rule of life—'the Law and the Prophets.'

It is not our business to comment at large on the most beautiful and striking verses of the Sermon on the Mount. We have only to note how they develop certain themes from the Lord's Temptations which the Our Father has already recalled so vividly. Jesus rejected in the wilderness Satan's offer of kingdoms and glories because it would involve a conflict of loyalties. 'The Lord thy God shalt thou worship, and him serve alone.' Christ could not accept a share in earthly empire at the price of compromise with idolatry. The Sermon makes a fresh point. Quite apart from any concession to paganism, the pursuit of lucre is itself idolatry, and comes under the same ban. 'No servant can serve two masters. If he does not hate the one and love the other, he will attend to one and neglect the other. You cannot serve God and Gain.' The rapacious Pharisee pilloried in a later text is free from any contact with heathendom; but still he is the idolater of gold. And, Jesus adds, though the pursuit of lucre is not heathenism, it is a heathenish business: 'After all these things do the gentiles seek' says Christ.

In preaching against worldly anxiety Jesus speaks of God's care for the birds. We may recall how Jesus had put himself in the wilderness among the creatures of the wild (so St. Mark had said); and how, when his fast and his trials were accomplished, the angels of God supplied his need. Had not God supplied Elijah in the wilderness, at one time by the ministry of an angel, at another by sending the birds of the air to drop him bread?

Jesus applies the almost legendary picture to the daily needs of his hearers. Their heavenly Father who feeds the birds knows that his human children have need of clothing and food. So, he says, 'seek first his kingdom and his righteousness, and all these things shall be added unto you.' Jesus rejected Satan's kingdom of earthly blessings for God's kingdom of righteousness; but material provision was added—angels ministered to his need. His hearers' lot is not cast in the wilderness, the divine Providence will not commonly employ the service of angels to sustain them. For the aim of promoting God's glory, and doing our duty as good men, has no general tendency to land us in physical starvation. But be that as it may, we are to put God's glory first, and banish anxiety by trusting a Father's love.

'All these things shall be added.' The student of scripture can scarcely read these words and not be reminded of Solomon, whose name, indeed, has been mentioned by Christ a few lines back. When God promised Solomon whatever boon he asked, he resisted the temptation to pray for wealth or regal splendour, after the manner of the kings of the world. He prayed for a discerning heart to judge the people of God; and this surely was 'to seek first the kingdom of God and his righteousness.' Yet God in granting his request added what he had not asked—all the wealth and royal honour his position called for. Yes—and even Solomon in all his glory, says Jesus, was not arrayed like any weed, when God clothes it with leaves and crowns it with flowers. Shall we make our principal anxiety a pittance of what came to Solomon in such abundance without his asking, and to the lilies of the field by mere nature?

If we go back to the Temptation-story with Christ's Sermon in our minds, we shall be led to see the Son's patient fasting as a silent supplication, which could not go unanswered. 'Ask, and you shall receive, seek, and you shall find. Every one that asks obtains, or that seeks, finds, and to him who knocks the door shall be opened. Is there a man among you who will give his son a stone when he asks him for bread?' The allusion to

Christ's temptation seems unmistakable here. Satan meant Jesus to feel that, in his need of bread, he was put off with stones; the Son would not believe that the stones were the Father's last word. 'Man shall not live by bread alone, but by every word that issues from the lips of God.' Certainly the answer to our prayer is not always in the form we intend; nevertheless the Father does not give us stones for bread. Jesus prayed in Gethsemane to be delivered from death. He was delivered through death, and glorified by resurrection.

Now that we have mentioned Gethsemane let us transfer our attention to it for a moment. For we can scarcely suppose that St. Matthew wrote the episode into his book without recalling the Lord's Prayer, and, behind the Lord's Prayer, the Temptation in the wilderness. *'My Father, if it be possible, let this cup pass from me—only not as I will, but as thou willest.'* (In the repetition a few lines below, we have the very words of the Lord's Prayer, *'Thy will be done'*),…'Watch and pray, *that ye enter not into temptation.'* The echoes are too plain to miss, even though the nature of the wilderness-temptation was, in a manner, opposite. There Jesus longed for wholesome bread, and consented to wait for it. Here he abhors the cup of bitterness, and consents to drink it. In both cases he accepts the harsh reality: the stones in the desert, the nails of the cross.

The echo of the Temptation does not end with the vigil in the garden; it continues through the crisis of the arrest; indeed we find ourselves advancing in due order from the theme of the first temptation to the theme of the second. For now, if ever, was the time to follow Satan's suggestion, and invoke the promise given to Messiah in the ninety-first psalm by calling on the assistance of the angels. But no; when one of Christ's twelve showed signs of fight, 'Put up your sword into its place' said Jesus. 'Do you doubt that I could beg my Father and have him send me here and now more than twelve regiments of angels? How then should the scriptures be fulfilled, which say that these things must be so?'

After the arrest, the bringing to judgment; and here we see the substance of the third temptation. The priests, failing in their first line of indictment, fall back on Christ's claim to be God's Anointed. Would he but compromise on the kingdom of God and accept the half-Jewish, half-heathen establishment, they have no case against him. But no, he will not give the devil his due, and he goes to Pilate's court, accused of treason against Caesar. Though he was no political rebel, he would not renounce the kingdom of God; he was crucified as king of the Jews. It had been Satan's lying boast, that an act of homage to himself would open to Jesus the kingdoms of the earth and all their glory; he spread them before Christ's eyes on that visionary mountain-top. The lies of Satan were outbidden by the truth of God when the crucified king of Israel met his disciples on a mountain appointed. 'All power' he said 'is given me in heaven and on earth. Go then, make disciples of all nations, teaching them to keep all that I commanded you. And lo, I am with you alway, to the end of the world.'

Jesus was tempted, and Satan was defeated in the wilderness. But the final temptation and the final victory belonged to Christ's passion at Jerusalem. By the strokes he has added to the story, St. Matthew shows us how the very pattern of the three conquests of Satan was repeated and fulfilled in the vigil, the arrest, and the execution of Jesus.

And that is where I propose to end. If I have any readers who complain that I have not edified them, or that I have broken off just when I ought to have drawn out the moral, I would suggest to them that they take up the Sermon on the Mount and consider it with these matters fresh in their minds.

Theologians may be no better at drawing morals than any one else; we have, as a tribe, been guilty of limitless impertinence in lecturing our betters; it is amazing how readily we have been forgiven. All we can reasonably claim is a specialty of learning, and it is this that I have tried to put at the disposal of my fellow-Christians. My book is for those who want to know what the evangelist was doing in writing the mysterious story that he wrote. I have done my best to explain it to them. I have tried not to plague them with irrelevant learning; I have concealed nothing essential and skated over no difficulties. I have told the truth as I see it.

I said at the beginning of the book that, to estimate the historical bearing of St. Matthew's story, one must first understand what he is saying to us. Now that I have explained the story as well as I can, am I to lay down the law on the degree of closeness with which it fits historical fact? No; here again I will refrain from the impertinence of telling my readers what to think. No level-headed person is likely to doubt that there are what our current jargon calls 'symbolical elements' in St. Matthew's story. The narrative has been more packed with meaning in every detail than a plain real-life story could possibly be. But in seeing how it reflects the mind and experience of Jesus, my readers may be wiser than I.

C OWLEY PUBLICATIONS is a ministry of the Society of St. John the Evangelist, a religious community for men in the Episcopal Church. Emerging from the Society's tradition of prayer, theological reflection and diversity of mission, the press is centered in the rich heritage of the Anglican Communion.

Cowley Publications seeks to provide books, audio cassettes, and other resources for the ongoing theological exploration and spiritual development of the Episcopal Church and other churches in the body of Christ. To this end, it is dedicated to developing a new generation of theological writers, encouraging them to produce timely, creative and stimulating publications of excellence, and making these publications available widely, reaching both clergy and lay persons.